I0105713

All In

Living, not Dying with ALS

A Journey of Faith

CHRIS BENYO

Inspired by Denise DiMarzo

Copyright © 2025 Chris Benyo.

All rights reserved. This book or any portion thereof may not be reproduced
or used in any manner whatsoever without the express written permission
of the publisher except for the use of brief quotation in a book review.

Leavitt Peak Press

ISBN: 978-1-967361-21-2 (sc)
ISBN: 978-1-967361-22-9 (e)

Rev. date: 04/03/2025

Foreword

This book traces the way my wife, Denise, lived with ALS, also known as Lou Gehrig's disease. I emphasize the word "lived" because I want her story to give hope to people with horrific diseases like ALS. Denise truly lived with it. This work will detail her experiences while living her life to the fullest despite the ravages of ALS. It will also document how I lived during this time, and I hope that my story will encourage caregivers around the world.

Because of Denise's incredible faith, she chose to live with ALS. This, in turn, gave me the strength I needed to be the best I could be as I cared for the love of my life. Without her faith, I don't know what might have happened.

By God's grace I have had the privilege of delivering speeches across the United States about our story, and various media outlets have taken notice (see Appendix for details). This book is a compilation of those presentations, interviews that we've done, Denise's riveting blog posts, and information that I've never shared in any public outlet. It will trace the arc of our lives from running races together, to me pushing Denise in a wheelchair while running marathons, to me now pushing an empty chair in remembrance of her as I compete.

Running is great, but running for a cause has been hands down better than I could have imagined. Interestingly enough, Denise's battle with ALS opened up a whole world of opportunity for us as we sought to raise awareness about this dreadful disease. In the pages that follow, I'll detail where that journey led us.

This is a story of love, of survival, and of running, the sport that united us and enables me to keep the memory of Denise alive. There's a lot to that empty chair, as you will discover in these pages.

I dedicate this book to my wonderful wife, Denise, who lives on after living well with ALS. May you, the reader, be as inspired as I was by this amazing woman.

CHAPTER 1
The News

The blog entry was from Tuesday, September 27, 2011, and it beautifully summarizes Denise's spirit, which I hope will infuse the pages of this book and inspire your soul.

It was simply titled "Introduction." Here is the text:

"Since I can't seem to manage to edit my profile successfully, this will serve as an introduction of sorts.

I consider myself to be just another ordinary person facing the challenges of physical limitations, albeit with strong determination, a heap of faith and a bit of humor.

My hope is to share my journey with you; instill faith in the belief that we are not in control, no matter what we think, and expose the joys, blessings and frustrations of adapting to the gradual loss of physical and sometimes emotional stability."

We see so much of Denise in so brief of a post, the self-deprecation, the bravery, the humility, the courage. I take issue with her description of herself as another ordinary person." She was anything but! Yet, that self-image is part of why I loved her so much. She truly did not see herself as special, but she was exceptional to me and many others.

I would want her to know that she absolutely fulfilled her wish in this first entry. She did face ALS "with strong determination, a heap of faith, and a bit of humor." She also was successful at instilling "faith in the belief that we are not in control, no matter what we think."

Her blog would go on to inform many about daily life with ALS. I believe it will educate and inspire many more for decades to come.

About six months after Denise and I were married, on December 9, 2010, to be exact, our faith was tested in a way we never could have imagined. In a dimly lit doctor's office these words were spoken: "You have ALS. There is no cure and no known treatment plan. It is a fatal disease. Life expectancy is two to five years after diagnosis. I'm sorry."

At this point a choice had to be made: Make the best of a terrible situation or wallow in self-pity. Choose to die with ALS or live with ALS and be all in. Because of Denise's incredible faith, she chose to live with ALS.

When I met Denise, she was in the best shape of her life. She exercised every morning and had just taken up running. I was twenty states into the 50 States Marathon Club. Denise and I began running together and even did several 5Ks together. I promised her on our wedding day, June 18, 2010, to run a marathon anywhere with her, provided she put in the training. I told her 5Ks were "cute," but nothing compared to the rush of finishing a marathon.

As we trained, some of the problems she was having were magnified and we had to stop. Then we got the diagnosis and life changed, in some ways, interestingly enough, for the better. My running gained a whole new dimension as I ran for a cause far greater than myself.

Before we would run together in a way that we never anticipated, Denise continued to come to grips with her new condition. The day after her first blog entry, she wrote "How it all started":

"While I'm sure everyone's experience is a bit different, the first sign of trouble began with random falls at Target. My husband and I loved to take a trip to Target on Sunday afternoons to pick up groceries and odds and ends; we called it Target Sunday. Yes, I know, life in the suburbs is so exciting, but we loved to spend the time alone together even if it was just at Target.

Back to the falling... It's not as if I was wearing heels and tripped over my clumsy feet; I'd come to describe it as: the upper half of my body was headed down the frozen foods aisle ready to select my favorite ice cream and someone forgot to tell my legs to join us. Down I'd go, slam! Mostly my hips would take the hit as I fell to one side or the other; the bruises were rather attractive.

Oftentimes I would have a Starbucks' Venti black coffee in hand for the event, as it was part of the Target Sunday ritual. It still perplexes the mind when I remember how often I fell without spilling a single drop. I'd land, coffee elevated high above my body like the Statue of Liberty holding her torch. This stunt played several times at the local Target, but still I dismissed it as nothing more than my habit of moving faster than necessary for any given task. Let's just say I had an East Coast pace in a Midwestern environment."

Again, we see Denise's bravery and humor, a charming mix that I never ceased to admire. I wish that we all could face difficult situations with such a combination of courage and seeing the lighter side of life.

Her description of these falls is poetic and incredibly accurate. It was as if her mind planned to go down one aisle and her body failed to get the order. When she fell, I fell a bit too. There's nothing like seeing your loved one accumulate bruises on her hips, that pointy bone that makes first contact with the unforgiving floors at Target. Neither of us appreciated ALS' incursion on one of our favorite times together each week. In some ways it was harder to watch her hurt herself than it was to have her body surrender later to a chair. This in-between time of mobility with fragility was frustrating and maddening, especially for an active couple like us.

I think it's one thing for a sedentary person to be afflicted with a disease that robs them of their ability to move. Such a person has lost very little. But someone who was motivated to train for marathons, as Denise was, lost a dear and precious capacity the ability to move often for extended periods of time. This made ALS that much harder to endure, yet Denise never stopped smiling. I can still see that smile and I am still amazed by it.

We see the trademark humor again in Denise's blog post two days later, entitled "Falling In Better Places..."

"Although Target seemed to be my favorite place to fall, before long I began to fall in even better places... There was the time when I was standing on line on a Monday morning around 7:30 am waiting to check in for a business conference at Caesar's Palace. Dressed in my conservative navy suit and pumps, trying to remain poised, I leaned a bit too far back and took the stanchions down with me like a row of dominos as I tumbled backward to the floor. My face turned red as I was pulled to my feet by a stranger, while others picked up the stanchions and still others looked on.

Later when I shared the story with my husband via phone, in an effort to console me, he remarked 'Don't worry about it, Honey; you're in Vegas, I'm sure they just thought you were drunk!'

Somehow, that didn't make me feel any less embarrassed, but it was amusing nonetheless.

That event was followed up a couple of weeks later with a tumble right out of the shower in a hotel room on another business trip, no witnesses... I could pretend it never happened, but when I fell with a thunderous thud as I clunked my head on the floor in my office and two of my coworkers rushed in to pick me up, I couldn't deny it."

As you can see, my attempts at humor could not rival Denise's. She touches on another cruel dimension of ALS, how it makes a fairly young and healthy businesswoman look like an elderly person who is trying to do too much. It's one thing to fall at Target with me right next to her; it was another thing to fall in the presence of strangers and coworkers, creating a different level of embarrassment. I know that must have hurt Denise deeply. It would hurt any human being, but she managed to laugh it off as best she could.

We were fully aware that ALS would embark on a long, progressive (or should I say "regressive"?) march, but that sort of medical knowledge does nothing to ease the pain of hitting your head on the office floor while your coworkers look at you with a mélange of pity and horror.

For Denise and I, sharing her diagnosis was something neither of us had looked forward to. When we were delivered the diagnosis, we (me more than her) cried the type of tears that aren't meant to be cried by anyone. Each tear takes a bit of your heart with it.

Denise stayed strong during the ride home and all I could do was try and figure out how to fix it. I'm a guy-that's what we do. Yet for me that does not translate into actual household fixing. I can't hammer a nail straight or use power tools. Quite honestly, they scare me. I can turn a 6-4-3 double play with the best of them and hit a lob wedge over a tree and watch it land on the green, but household stuff and cars leave me a bit challenged. Scratch that. I don't even try. They have people to do that type of stuff, right? What's the difference between a Phillips head and straight-head screwdriver again?

Anyway, I just knew that I could "fix" this ALS thing for the love of my life. I was her husband. I was supposed to fix things and protect her from everything-even terminal diseases. As we came to discover, there was no "fixing it." So much for me riding up on my white horse in a white ten-gallon hat to save the day. I so wish I could have done more.

The first order of business was to tell our neighbors two doors down. After all, they had been watching Denise's daughter Maddie while we were at the doctors. They opened the door, and I immediately lost it. How Christa got Maddie out without seeing this bawling baby, I don't know. Lori didn't say anything. She just held me close and let me sob away. Thanks, Lori. It was exactly what I needed at the time.

After Maddie was put to bed, Denise finally allowed the magnitude of her diagnosis to sink in. She sobbed and I held her. Throughout all of this ALS ride, Denise never asked anything much of me. On that night she asked me if I would stay home from work the next day. Of course, I did, and we sobbed, hugged, and held on to each other all day long.

I managed to hold off telling my incredible work family at Meadow Glens School for several weeks. Looking back, I know they knew something was up, but staying true to form, they left me alone until I got the courage to tell them. Of course, I had told my close friends and my principal. He handled it with grace and said, "Whenever you want to tell the staff, I'll call a brief meeting."

When I finally summoned up the courage to tell my staff, I was again stunned by this group of people I work with every day. Every person showed up in the art room to support me: teachers, administrators, aides, assistants, and even one of the custodians. This was not a mandatory meeting. I never would have made it one.

All Chuck said was "Chris has something to share," and they all came. Can I say I am blessed?

On that day in the art room I told everyone what we were dealing with. Of course, I again wept like a baby and lots of other tears flowed in that room that day, along with hugs and gestures of support. I am a lucky man to have been surrounded by such great people.

And their love and support didn't stop there. They continued to show up for the entire ALS experience. I love every one of the people I work with, and one day I will tell them all what they mean to me. Perhaps that will be communicated in this book somehow.

I can't really speak for how Denise revealed the news to her friends and colleagues. I will say this: her office stepped up big time when she informed them.

She was a valuable member of the team and they didn't hesitate to let her know it.

One of her friends took over the responsibility of getting Denise to work. It was out of her way but she did it with a smile on her face. The office also came together and made meals for us, not just mac 'n' cheese, either, I'm talking gourmet meals. The owner himself purchased a scooter for Denise to get around at work and also made a call to the Mayo Clinic on her behalf. Consequently, she got in within days for a second opinion.

I do know that Denise told everyone in a way that didn't make them sad, at least in Denise's presence they weren't sad. Everyone who Denise told knew beyond a shadow of a doubt that ALS had a huge fight on its hands, a formidable opponent: my wonderful wife. There was no quit in my beautiful Italian spouse--and people took their cues from her, including me. In that way, the entire experience was nothing short of amazing.

CHAPTER 2

People

One of the ironies of dealing with a terminal illness is that instead of narrowing your circle of friends and cutting you off from others, it can--and should--actually bring you into the orbit of scores of impressive people who will show you love and care beyond what you've ever experienced. This shower of love, from small favors to huge efforts, proved to be one of the most profound blessings that we experienced during our battle with ALS. Frankly, the kindness of others over the past half-dozen years changed my life and outlook forever.

I do not have enough room in these pages to cite every person by name who intervened in a meaningful way in our lives, but Denise hailed many of them in her blog entries and other articles. I'd like to describe a few of our heroes and benefactors too. As you read about them, don't just admire them; find the necessary motivation to help those in need around you.

As you read the following pages, I also hope that you will be deeply encouraged about our world and the type of people who live in it. Our planet is not just filled with meanness and self-centeredness, no matter what the daily headlines blare. No, scores of people live and walk among us who are ready to get outside of themselves and sacrifice, just to help us get through life, from total strangers to rock-solid family members. We need to return the favor. We need to be channels of TLC as well. We need to give as we have received. Even as I write that sentence, I know I will never be able to effectively repay the folks described in this chapter.

And guess what? They don't care. They didn't love us to receive thanks. That's the definition of "selfless."

Denise summarized the widespread care of others for us in a beautifully written article that she submitted to Ladies Home Journal:

They say that victims of earthquakes experience them in slow motion; as the walls come crashing down around them in minutes, time seems to stand still. Sitting with my husband in the doctor's office after months of searching for answers, I had a similar experience when the neurologist delivered my diagnosis of amyotrophic lateral sclerosis (ALS), commonly known as Lou Gehrig's disease. The words hung in the air, as if I had the option to dismiss them or accept them. I remained calm, almost frozen, as I noticed the tears begin to stream down my husband's face. 'Two to five years,' the doctor said, 'That's the prognosis for this disease. There's no cure, no effective treatment for what you have, I'm sorry.'

I had heard of Lou Gehrig's disease, but frankly I knew nothing about it. I was always concerned about Multiple Sclerosis, as it runs in my family, so when my symptoms began to progress, I was almost certain MS would be the conclusive diagnosis. I was prepared for that, not for ALS, not for something worse, not for something fatal. In the days to follow, I remember thinking, why isn't there a cure or at the very least an effective treatment?

Unfortunately, like an earthquake, when we hear about ALS, it only lasts a news cycle and then we lose focus, but the devastation remains.

And then come the aftershocks, as you tell your family and close friends, your boss, co-workers, and eventually the person who cleans your home, cuts your hair, and paints your nails, because you can no longer hide the fact that you're sick.

Each time it becomes more real, more terrifying, and more overwhelming, until you decide to accept it and live your life despite it! Today I am living with-not dying with-ALS.

I don't say this flippantly, like someone in denial, and I didn't get here easily, but I did get to a place of hope and optimism because of the people that surround me.

In my twenties I read a book about family systems; the author used a mobile to illustrate how an event in the life of just one member of the family will impact every other member of that family system. Try it: watch a mobile moving effortlessly in synchronized harmony, now touch just one of those dangling pieces and the next thing you see is utter chaos, each piece flying through the air in a different direction. You see, the expectation is that there is always a negative impact; that has not been my experience; that is not my story.

As I sit here in my power wheelchair, feeling the warmth of the afternoon sunlight on my face, I am reminded that spring is coming. Each year, when I think that I just can't take another day of winter's biting cold, spring pops and a daffodil breaks the earth's crust and pushes through. This is one of my favorite things. It's the way I've come to think about living with my disease... Just when I think I can't endure another day, something happens to remind me there are good days still ahead.

Days when I get to share lunch with friends, see musicals at the theater, receive a note of encouragement from a dear friend I haven't seen in 20 years, and recently I got to see my beautiful ten-year-old daughter sing 'You Make My Dreams Come True' on stage while she literally was making my dreams for her come true. Her joy was my joy!

Since early 2010 I have experienced what it's like to move from an active working mom who exercised daily, enjoyed rollerblading, cycling, cross country skiing and running with her husband and children, to a mom that has learned to use assistive technology in order to help her daughter do her 4th grade math homework because I could no longer speak. That said, if not for my illness, I would not have been home after school with her to spend those precious moments.

What I have learned in the past few years as my body gradually deteriorated is that being sick is not for those weak in spirit. It takes determination, strong faith and the ability to see the blessings that come along with the pain, to get through it one day, one hour, and sometimes one minute at a time.

Most importantly, I've seen how my illness has impacted those around me. Over the last three years I have seen co-workers, friends, and neighbors become my hands and feet when mine would no longer serve me. They provided child care, transportation and meals when we needed them. They packed up our things and unpacked them again to move us into a new home when I could no longer climb the stairs of our family's home. They participated in walkathons and ran alongside us, as my husband pushed me in a specially designed jogger, to honor a commitment he made to run my first marathon. A special group of neighbors even went door to door to tell our story and raise awareness and funding for research and patient care.

Just when we thought we had seen blessing after blessing, two former students of my husband's, now in junior high school, organized an annual dodgeball tournament. Recruiting support from local businesses, parents, fellow students, and teachers to help, these young ladies engaged the entire community in our efforts to fight!

Greatest blessing in this 5-year battle with ALS.

They've organized the dodgeball tournament for two years now, and each time I roll into the high school field house, I am overwhelmed by the number of people who participate and attend. There were teams of teachers, parents, high school students, and junior high students, each team dressed to show their unique spirit, each more amusing than the next! Bubble wrapped teachers, moms in tiaras, and students in their brightly colored t-shirts and wild socks, they made me smile and laugh.

My Schools Dodgeball Team 2015. Denise's last tournament.
Sporting hot pink as that was Denise's favorite color.

Many of them greeted me or stopped by to ask how I was doing, and reminded me that they keep us in their prayers. One adorable group of tiny elementary school girls, who attend the school my husband works in, walked by the bleachers back and forth, selling wristbands, stopped by to ask about my new puppy, Sally.

Apparently, word got out about my furry Valentine's Day gift! I did not have my Dynavox (communication device) yet, so it was difficult to respond, but I smiled and nodded my head to acknowledge them, and mouthed the words, 'Thank you.'

I also had the pleasure of meeting the lovely young ladies who inspired us with their vision for the event, along with their parents, grandparents, and siblings.

One family who participated had recently lost their high-school-aged son, Michael, to brain cancer. Yet Mom was at the front table welcoming people as they entered the event, collecting admission, and Dad led a team, The Heavy Hitters. Both greeted me individually, and although there was little spoken dialogue, I sensed a connection of deep understanding in their eyes, a moment of mutual compassion that won't be erased from my heart. My husband had been one of Michael's teachers, and even in their time of grief, they were present to support us, nothing short of amazing.

This was impact we never saw coming! This was community at its best, and I am humbled, and filled with gratitude, because no matter how bad it gets, we are not alone."

Now you see what I mean about Denise living with ALS, not allowing it to keep her from enjoying the last years she had with us. It was indeed incredible how people came through for us in myriad ways, and their efforts continue as they impact my life in many ways.

One special group of people that rushed to our aid were the staff and students at Meadow Glens School, where I have taught physical education for eighteen years. This school, as well as the entire district, stepped up in support of us beyondwhat Denise or I could ask or think. For instance, during the summer of the ALS Ice Bucket Challenge in 2014, literally hundreds of people performed this simple gesture for Denise and my benefit, with many schools participating at all grade levels, from K-12. Even the district office personnel took freezing ice baths for us.

Honestly, I never saw such support coming.

One facet of that ice bucket phenomenon that moved me to tears occurred just before the school year started that late summer. Two days before the kick-off day for classes, I half-seriously challenged my school to take on the challenge. If you're not a teacher, you'll never understand how stressful those days can be before the academic year starts. Everyone is moving in one hundred different directions as we prepare for our new students.

I figured a handful of my closest friends would participate in the challenge because that's how they rolled. To my amazement, when I ventured outside for the challenge, my entire school was in line with a bucket to participate. It happened to fall on Denise's birthday; I was moved to tears (which happens a lot, as you can tell).

The word got out that day about the massive show of solidarity, and many of my students' families came to school to watch and cheer us on. It was one of many beautiful sights that I took in during these dark years. The following Halloween my school's equivalent of the PTA took the challenge for us as well, not letting freezing weather stop them from conveying their concern for us in a real (and sacrificial) way.

I'll never be able to thank the group of outstanding professionals in my school district enough for what they meant to us. They were a large part of God's enormous blessing to us during this journey.

Here's another example of the remarkable love and support that we received from my school. Denise referred to a dodgeball tournament in her post above.

Here's the backstory:

One fall afternoon I got an e-mail from a parent asking if she, her daughter, and her daughter's close friend could stop by school to see me. Taylor and Delaney were in seventh grade at the time. I had taught them from K-5 at Meadow Glens.

They were taking a social studies class that required a service project. They could have gone to a soup kitchen or homeless shelter to get the needed hours, but they had another idea.

They had heard about our story on Facebook and wanted to do something.

They asked me if they could hold a dodgeball tournament to raise funds and awareness for ALS. Being a teacher, I asked them, "Why?" You know, probing questions-it's a teacher thing. What they said next shook me to my core. As if they had rehearsed it, they said in unison: "We wanted to do something for someone who matters to us." With tears in my eyes, The First Annual Dodgin' for Lou Gehrig's

Dodge Ball Tournament was born.

(See http://www.dodgin4lougehrigs.com/ for details.)

Taylor and Delaney are both seniors in high school now and have made such a difference over the past several years. They tell me how inspired they have been by Denise's grace, strength, and faith; and they attribute the tournament's steady growth to her character and legacy. If any kids read this, I have this message for you: don't let anyone tell you, you can't do something. Taylor and Delaney were seventh graders when this started, and they will soon surpass the $100,000 mark in total donations accumulated over the past half-dozen years. These young ladies have been an immense bright spot for me and many others! Who can you help and serve today? You never know where it will lead.

Another prominent role that caregivers played in our lives was picking us up when we were down. ALS can certainly haul you on a deep dive into your lowest emotions, but our unofficial support team helped us swim out of the blues again and again. Denise wrote about this in a blog post called, appropriately, "Blessings."

It's another great example of how others carried us through our battle in ways large and small. Don't ever underestimate the power of even a seemingly insignificant act of kindness. I know I never will again.

"This is for my neighbor... He and his wife and two small children live at the top of the block. Just this fall his daughter entered Kindergarten and so now we have another child taking the school bus, who lives on our side of the busy street we need to cross to get to the bus stop. Stay with me...it will begin to make sense as to why these matters.

Anyway, I can use my scooter to accompany my daughter up to the end of the block to watch her cross the street and get on the bus, but admittedly there are days I don't feel up to the task. While those days are few and far between, I beat myself up over the idea of letting her go alone. I was raised with a healthy dose of good old Italian Catholic guilt, so it's easy for me to fall into this trap. Over and over, I repeat the rules on how to safely cross the street, in case one day I cannot muster the strength to go with her, but it's difficult for me to be okay with this kind of independence.

A few days into the school year I noticed my neighbor and his daughter began to use the school bus service, and so while we waited for the bus, they joined us on the corner. We made fast friends of them, because my daughter cannot imagine anyone who wouldn't be delighted to talk with her, and she started right in asking them questions so she could get to know them. Although his daughter was shy and mostly hid behind him, Dad was tolerant of her inquiries and friendly.

After a few days, when they reached the corner, he turned to my daughter and said,

'Shall we cross?' and she hugged me goodbye and crossed safely with them. When the bus left and he returned to our side of the street, I thanked him, offered up the customary 'Have a good day!' and we parted ways to head back to our homes.

Since that day, I've come to notice that they wait to cross the street until we arrive, and I take comfort in knowing she won't be crossing alone if one day I don't feel up to the task. I'm embarrassed to say that I don't know your name, but thank you, neighbor, for stepping up and making a mom feel a little less worried.

In case you're out there and you read this…Do you like brownies? I'd like to bake you some…"

I could fill a library with stories about the kindness of neighbors, and even strangers, as we faced down ALS. This post is emblematic of the type of simple gestures that people made in response to Denise's neediness. Honestly, watching how the vast majority of people cared for us during this time was enough to restore my faith in humanity. From waiting to cross the street so that Denise did not have to travel the entire circuit on her scooter, to gathering around her chair for a hug before a marathon, I get teary-eyed just thinking of how many people reached out to us and showed that they cared. In short, they loved us—and we desperately needed love. Denise and I drank it in, and I still draw on those reserves when my day gets tough and I risk plunging into sadness.

When I finally admitted that I couldn't do this alone the whole situation changed. During our journey, Denise and I talked about being blessed in so many ways. I feel the biggest blessing God bestowed on us was the four primary caregivers that helped us endure this difficult passage of life. I feel it very important to mention them, if only briefly. I could not and did not do this myself. I thought I could but I was so wrong. Thank God for the caregivers that showed up almost magically to help us and make Denise's five-year-plus battle beautiful. Let me tell you about a few angels who came into our lives undisguised:

Laura was a neighbor of ours in Bartlett, Illinois. One day, Denise fell when I was not home, but she managed to call Laura, who came over to help. From that day forward Laura cared for Denise in the early stages of ALS. I didn't even know Laura until one day I came home and there she was, like a modern-day Florence Nightingale. Thank you, Laura. You helped immensely in the early stages of our battle with ALS.

A few years into the struggle we decided that I needed some night help. My sleeping had been sporadic at best, which obviously affected the care that I could give to Denise. Thus, an ad was drawn up and sent to various colleges in the area.

Along came Jess, a nursing student at Aurora University. She provided much-needed assistance a few nights a week and was simply incredible-supremely confident and skilled. One day when Denise was rushed to the hospital, Jess stepped up big time. I don't know what I would have done without her. Thank you, Jess. You, too, are an angel.

As ALS progressed, caring for Denise became very difficult for Laura. She tried valiantly, but helping Denise became too hard. In came Brandi, seemingly out of the blue. Talk about God working in mysterious ways! Brandi was the niece of one of the night custodians at my school. He knew I was looking for help, gave me Brandi's number, and Denise clicked with her immediately at the interview. This was crucial because life got exceedingly difficult-yet Brandi answered the call beautifully. Brandi was phenomenal right up to the end; she knew exactly what to do to make Denise's last days comfortable. Thank you, Brandi, for all you did.

The fourth angel was named Talia, who was best friends with Jess, and also a nursing student at Aurora University. When Jess got a new job, Talia filled our need for a night caregiver. Are you kidding me? What are the chances of that-finding an equally capable caregiver who was close friends with the previous one?

Again, there was an immediate bond; Denise and Talia grew extraordinarily close.

Talia was gentle, smart, and loved Jesus just as much as Denise did. Denise's infectious smile was always on her face when Talia was around. Thank you, Talia.

I'm forever in your debt as well.

God blessed us with the caregivers we were fortunate to have. They were the epitome of God's hands and feet and a massive blessing.

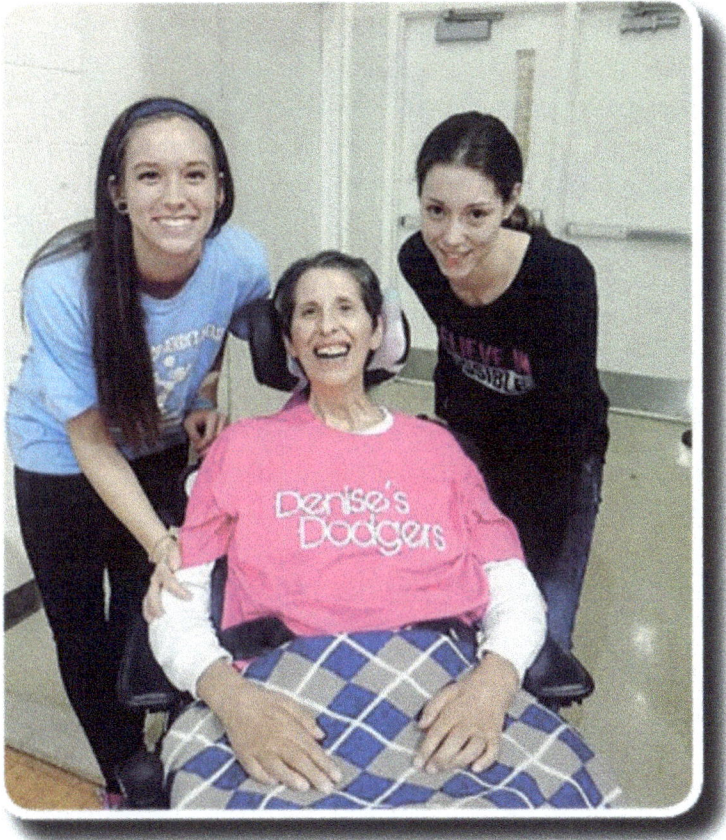

Denise and her caregivers at last year's Dodgeball Tournament. Talia on the left and Brandi on the right.

Two incredible blessings. My favorite picture of those 3.

One final note: Aurora University College of Nursing, keep doing what you're doing! If Jess and Talia were indicative of the type of nurses you are turning out, then the field of nursing will be set for a long time. Thank you for all you do.

Along with these caregivers, ALS caused our paths to cross with a multitude of people we might never have had the privilege of encountering, were it not for our dilemma. Among those people were fellow ALS-sufferers who encouraged us in an empathetic way that no one else could match, obviously. Joe, a neighbor we probably would have never met were it not for ALS, was one of the fellow warriors that cheered our souls. Denise wrote about him in October 2011 as she kept up a healthy pace of posting. "May God Bless Joe" again reveals Denise's kind heart, always wishing the best for others, never giving in to the temptation of schadenfreude. It also reminded us of just how small the world can be.

"Just yesterday afternoon we were out in front of the house watching our eight-year-old daughter master riding her bike without training wheels for the very first time... and out of nowhere appeared Joe. Admittedly, we were distracted as we wanted to capture the moment, but Joe was unaware of the accomplishment, and so he strolled over as if it were just another day.

Oddly, we had never met Joe before, but he was interested in chatting so we politely indulged him while keeping an eye on our priority. 'That's a nice scooter you have there...they run between $2000 and $3000,' he said. 'Oh, I really don't know about that; this was a gift,' I replied. 'Well, it's a nice one, and I may need one myself; I'll find out soon!' Joe responded. His comment just begged to be acknowledged, so I took the bait. 'May I ask why?' 'Well,' he said, 'I have a degenerative neuromuscular disease...' and the conversation stole my attention.

Could it really be true? The man standing before me, a man I'd never met, who lives right down the street, is also afflicted with ALS? Well, yes, apparently so... only Joe can walk, and his speech is just fine and he denied any issues with breathing and swallowing. He described his unique presentation of the disease as Flailing Arms, which after further investigation via the internet, I learned was called Brachial Amyotrophic Diplegia, a form of ALS that may or may not turn into full-blown ALS.

Joe explained that he's had it for six years and that it has only affected his hands and arms. When he extended his arms toward me, I could see the misshapen hands he held out, looked hollowed in the same places as mine, his fingers curled as the tendons tightened, and the muscles in his arms were mostly gone. It was all too familiar; he indeed had some form of ALS.

He shared that he was participating in a study with Dr. Siddique, a neuroscientist with Northwestern's Feinberg School of Medicine, who recently announced his discovery of the cause of ALS. We were well aware of Dr. Siddique and the discovery; it has given us hope and now we learned that Joe down the street was donating spinal fluid, blood and tissue samples to help find a cure.

There are roughly 35,000 registered cases of ALS in the U.S. on any given day, and it is believed that there may be as many as 300,000 cases internationally.

So... May God Bless Joe, who can still walk, and talk, and breathe; I pray he won't ever need a scooter."

Another kindhearted Joe in our lives was a colleague of Denise's. During one dark period of fear and worry, Joe came through for us in a way that we will never forget. He was never an "average Joe" for us, and you should never see yourself as one when you serve others in practical, unspectacular ways. Denise details Joe's ministry to us in this blog post, entitled: "Wow! Mom, His Name is in the Food."

"There are so many ways in which our family has been cared for these past ten months, I could easily write for days as I acknowledge those who have foundthoughtful ways to show us their support. This post is for one of those dear friends, Sloppy Joe!

Now, don't get the wrong impression, Joe is not a sloppy guy; in fact, he is one of the most meticulous people I know. One day, I was rummaging through a box of files from a project launch that was accomplished nearly ten years ago, searching for some detailed information, and I found the lunch order for the team who was working on the project, complete with names, sandwich orders, and important condiment preferences like: with or without mayo noted. Joe has always been very thorough.

Joe also knows that juggling school-aged kids, getting homework done, running a household, and holding a full-time job leaves parents feeling like they ran a marathon most days. Add to that equation a parent with physical limitations or an illness, and you ve got even greater challenges.

I learned a lot from Joe over the years both personally and professionally. I used to chuckle when he could tell me precisely how long it took for one of his boys to brush his teeth, and how many minutes he had to quiz them in the car on the way to school, to be sure they were prepared for the weekly spelling tests. He had the routine down to a science, and before long I found myself using these strategies to run my own daily marathon.

Although Joe had so much on his plate already, he often took the time to prepare an extra batch of whatever meal he was preparing for his own family and bring it in for me to take home to my family. Complete with salad, sides, bread, dessert, and heating instructions carefully taped to the main dish, Joe delivered several delicious, kid-friendly meals!

My family raved about all of the dinners, and especially loved his Ghirardelli brownies with the chocolate chunks, but my favorite response came from our youngest the first time he made us Sloppy Joes. Wow! Mom, his name is in the food! She was clearly impressed!

Joe, this one's for you! Thank you for the many delicious meals; you will always come to mind whenever we have Sloppy Joe's..."

Another source of TLC was not a special human, but a dog, a dog named Blue. One theme that you will find as you study the lives of people who struggle with life-threatening disease is the key role that their pets often play in their lives.

Denise was a cat fan for most of her life. She came to understand how we dog fans see life through her relationship with Blue. In a couple of blog posts, Denise discusses the role that pets played in her life. Here is the first, entitled: "My Boy Blue."

"It's likely that some of you will conjure up a scene from the movie 'Old School' with Will Ferrell crying out, 'You're my boy, Blue!' when stumbling upon the title of this post. We hear this all the time when people learn our dog's name, Blue.

Personally, not being a huge Will Ferrell fan, I must admit I had to Google the phrase before I knew what people were talking about. While I can watch "Elf" repeatedly at Christmas time, I considered agreeing to see "Talladega Nights," penance for the occasional chick flick!

When my husband and I married and combined households, I have to confess I was not 100% sold on the idea of having a dog come live with us. No offense to dogs in general, or to Blue specifically. You see, I grew up with dogs as pets and loved having them.

However, I've spent most of my adult life sharing my home with felines. Not because I liked them any better, they just fit into my lifestyle better, being career oriented and often maintaining a fairly aggressive schedule.

Dogs need to be walked and cats came potty trained; it was a no-brainer for me.

Although not as rewarding, I had been a cat owner for the last twenty-three years. I say cat owner because I don't wish to be labeled a 'Cat Person'; I am an animal lover. Let's be clear about this, because the stereotypical Cat Person is weird and everyone knows that...Please don't send me any nasty-grams on this subject.

Where was I... ok, so here we are getting married, we each have one child, good that works out, we each have a treadmill... that might be tight but we can work it out and oh...? I have two cats and you have a dog. I might not have been 100% on board but I'm no idiot, and I am not going to be the evil stepmother who would not take the dog in... so we may need to pay for cat therapy sessions but let's give it a try.

So, Blue joined us and the cats hid for about three months... and when Blue was in his crate they came out, ate, used the litter box and sauntered by the crate just to let Blue know they were still in charge!

Have you ever noticed that dogs come willingly when called, tails wagging, ready to slobber all over you, and cats sit there looking at you as if to say 'So, if I come, what's in it for me?' Well, my cats aren't really like that; they're downright needy and I'm pretty certain Nik thinks he's a dog. So, after a few months we all learned to live peacefully together. That's not to say there isn't an occasional chase...but in general they co-exist in harmony.

The funniest part about it is the jealousy; it's gotten to the point that when I call the cat, the dog rushes over, and it's not uncommon to have all three of them on you at once.

So… this post is for my boy Blue, who has wormed his way into my heart by following me from room to room, watching to see that I'm ok, and taking every opportunity to slobber all over my face whenever he gets the chance. You are my loving companion, and I wouldn't want to be on this journey without you…"

My Boy Blue. Denise's protector and wanna be Lap Dog.

In addition to Blue, we had a cat that Denise adored and then a third member of the menagerie that had Denise wishing that there would be puppies in heaven.

That was, in fact, the name of this blog post, written in May 2013, well into Denise's deterioration due to ALS.

"Sometimes it seems like a three-ring circus around here, but I wouldn't trade it for anything! If you've been reading my blog, then you already know about Blue, our 50-pound Border Collie mix who thinks he's a lap dog. Given the chance, Blue would gladly sit on my lap, if he could just figure out how to get up here without hurting either of us. Luckily, he has not found a way.

Then there's Crabby, our cat. She has earned her name with her 'Don't call us, we'll call you!' attitude. Don't misunderstand, she wants attention, it's just going to be on her terms, and not yours. You cannot pick her up, you cannot brush her, or move her, unless she approves. Weighing in at about ten pounds, I am often amazed at the effort it takes to get her to budge.

She is a beautiful long haired, grey and white kitty, with bright, hazel green eyes.

Unfortunately, if she won't let you brush her coat, it becomes matted, and since that was my job, well... you get the picture. Recently, we had her groomed into a lion cut. It's exactly what you would imagine, she was shaved with the exception of her head in the shape of a lion's mane, and what appears to be a duster at the tip of her tail, simply hilarious! I'd imagine she's feeling a bit naked, having lost much of her body mass in the process!

She has taken to new behaviors as a result of the whole traumatic event: sleeping on the heating vents, my right shoulder during naps or overnight, and walking the length of the edge of the whirlpool tub, as if it were a balance beam, to jump on my lap during my therapies in the morning. Not that I mind so much, but she's disconnected my feeding tube a couple of times now, and that's a big mess!

Overall, I'd have to say, she has been a lot cuddlier. She was living in the basement for about six months after we moved, and she has finally moved up to the main floor to live with the rest of the family. I still don't think that she's forgiven us, but it's nice to see her back.

Then after years of pleading, my wish came true on Valentine's Day, and my dear husband placed a ball of fur on my lap, later known as Sally or officially, Mustang Sally Brown, on her pedigree papers. She is the cutest thing on four feet! Golden and white, the most adorable menace you've ever met. Living up to her breeding, she's a little Shih... Tzu much of the time!

Nothing is safe anymore, Sally drags around whatever she can get to: slippers, shoes, towels, and unmentionables of all kinds. She loves to play in the backyard, hops through the grass like a bunny, and enjoys trudging through the flower beds to find a stick to chew on in the mulch. Sally doesn't subscribe to the idea of being a little lady, and returns looking like a scruffy mutt, enveloped in dirt! The only thing to do at that point, is to drop her into the laundry room tub. My husband seems to enjoy it and so does she, especially the blow dry to follow.

Blue and Sally are great together, rolling around on the floor, chasing each other, sharing their toys in a tug of war, and terrorizing the cat; they were fast friends.

They have brought me so much joy and endless amusement, the very best medicine.

I feel a strong connection to our pets; I'm certain Blue knew I was sick well before we did. He is on the job 24 hours a day, even when I make the slightest noise in the still of the night, he is up on the bed investigating. There was even a time I recall him waking my husband in the middle of the night, when I attempted to get up on my own, as if to say 'Hold on, you're not going anywhere alone.' My protector.

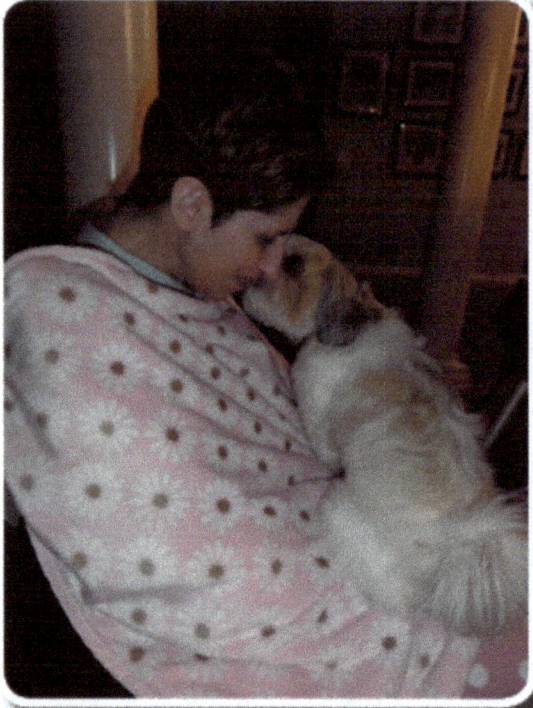

Pets are God's little bundles of healing energy, and
I sure hope there are puppies in heaven..."

Denise's Valentine's Day Present. Sally giving one of her many kisses. A real Lap Dog. Sorry Blue.

I'm not sure about puppies, but I'm sure that many of the people who sacrificed their time, energy, and comfort to minister to us will be in heaven.

Denise returned to the theme of thanking those who loved on us throughout our journey in a post appropriately titled "Angels in Our Midst." Read it and be encouraged.

"It's easy to see blessings when you set your mind to the positive, and so I've been taking time to identify and acknowledge these in a daily gratitude journal.

Sometimes the entries are simple things like an unexpected note, a phone call or visit from a friend or family member, and sometimes they are entries about the people I would have never met if not for my illness.

Strangers who demonstrated: kindness, compassion, hope and encouragement, just when I needed it most. Although I may only name a few here, know that there have been many in the past year, and as each day passes more of them appear along the way.

Dearest Pauline, you are filled with light and healing energy, and through you I have gained peace and the capacity to be gentle with myself. Thank you for your guidance and healing.

Holly, thank you for permission to allow myself to grieve and fall to pieces, when everyone around me always expects me to be strong, including the worst offender--me... Thank you for the encouragement to journal and embrace the journey.

Robert, I feel so fortunate that you did not see my disease as an obstacle to healing my shoulder. The pain began in January, and by September when you came to help me, it was frozen and immobile. I thought I would never regain the strength or range of motion to use my arm again. You gave me hope, encouragement and the will to fight through the pain.

It's sad to say, but when you have ALS, most of the medical professionals you encounter are focused on educating you on the progression of the disease and helping you prepare for what's to come as you digress. It's rare to find someone who encourages you to fight! Thank you, Robert, for your positive spirit and faith in me.

Laurie, from the day we met, I felt as if I'd known you for years. Thank you for your visits and listening as I babble endlessly... Your practical insights help me stay on track.

And… Joe, the neighbor just down the street, who may have never come by to meet us if he did not recognize that we shared the same challenging disease. Thank you for checking on me this week and bringing me hope in the form of new research information you gathered at a recent ALS seminar I could not attend.

To all of the angels in our midst, it's likely that our paths would not have crossed if not for my situation, but my life has been impacted by your presence, my faith made stronger, and my heart has been touched, and for that I am truly grateful…"

I've mentioned my coworkers at length, but Denise had a remarkably caring support team at her workplace as well. We talked often about the care we received from coworkers and wondered aloud if we would have done the same if the roles were reversed. As you read Denise's blog post entitled "Uncommon People," be challenged to be an uncommon person as well.

"Twelve years ago this month, I began working at a family-owned business in the height of their busiest time of the year, the holiday season. The atmosphere was a bit crazed at the time, since they had just gone live with their new ERP system and well.the organization was reeling from strong growth and adapting to both organizational and functional changes. I wasn't sure about what I stepped into at the time but I soon realized how fortunate I was…This was no ordinary workplace, and these were not ordinary people.

Over the years, I was blessed to have the opportunity to grow and learn through challenging assignments, and the rewarding experience of encouraging others to achieve their potential. I worked with a team of people who were capable, responsible and resourceful, and they had a unique talent for using humor to diffuse stress. I also had the privilege of developing lasting friendships and getting to know the people I worked with and their families.

The business was a good combination of large enough to provide challenge and growth, yet small enough for everyone to be known for their strengths and contributions. It was not unusual for the owner or CEO to greet staff members by name while passing them in the hallways. It had the feel of being home to me for many years. This, in of itself, made it difficult to accept the fact that the progression of my disease would eventually force me to give it up much sooner than I wanted.

While the physical changes were gradual, it did become apparent that something was wrong by the end of 2010, and although my co-workers didn't pry, they began to show concern, and offer assistance when I needed it. Those closest to me knew of our pursuit to figure out what was causing these changes in my physical condition, and when we confirmed the diagnosis, the word began to get out.

I will never find words to accurately describe the overwhelming support and caring I experienced in this organization, from the owner, CEO and Executive Team, to those in my group, and others, outside of my group, with whom I rarely worked.

They were kind and generous beyond any expectation. One incredibly bigheartedindividual provided a scooter that made it safer for me to get around in the building. Co-workers held doors, waited patiently for me to pass, and smiled or joked with me to normalize what could otherwise be awkward.

They sent personal notes, cards and thoughtful gifts, offered prayers, made meals for us, took me to lunch and even doctor's appointments. One special family drove out of their way to take me to and from work for eight months, often treating me to a Starbuck's venti black coffee on the drive in. They carried my bags, my lunch, my walker, and let me grab onto them, as I moved slowly to get in and out of the building.

When we formed a team to participate in the walk for ALS, they mobilized a fundraising effort that collected thousands of dollars in donations to support ALS patients and their families, most of which came from their own pockets. They additionally provided donations for any equipment I might personally need.

This is no ordinary company, and these are not ordinary people; they have been my family for a long time, and this is only one example of how they take care of their own.

I can identify with what Lou Gehrig was feeling when he gave his "Luckiest Man on the Face of the Earth" speech at Yankee Stadium, because for the last twelve years it has been an honor to work with such a fine group of people, and for that I am truly grateful."

I'll close this chapter with one of Denise's final posts that still gets me choked up. Despite her substantial physical limitations, she powered through and was determined to thank the many people who helped her to perform even simple tasks as her body rebelled and refused to do so.

Who needs your help at work? In your neighborhood? In your house of worship? Use posts like this to inspire you to make a difference, to die to self a little bit and brighten the world of someone near you. That's what Denise would want if she were here today.

Here's "Dear Friends and Family," posted April 5, 2013, more than three years into the journey of living with ALS:

"As many of you know, I have been living with ALS, Lou Gehrig's disease, since my symptoms began in early 2010. It's now been three years since this all began, and I have learned a lot about myself, and the incredible people who have been right beside me.

When it began my fingers were twitching and losing strength, and you helped me open my water bottles. When my right leg started to drag, you laughed with me and told me it was time to give up wearing heels. When I fell and broke my wrist, you started driving me to work, bought me a cane, and eventually a scooter to get around safely. When my speech began to slur, and it strained me to talk, you spoke for me. When I received my diagnosis, you held me in your arms and cried with me.

When I could not come to work, you visited me, and when I could not climb down the stairs of my home you helped move me to a handicap-accessible home. You walked alongside my husband and I in walkathons, and many of you cheered, walked, and ran with us in my first marathon!

Together, with your help we raised over 50,000 dollars for research and patient care in the last two years! An unbelievable accomplishment that our patient community recognizes with immeasurable gratitude. I see firsthand the benefits of your fundraising efforts right in our local support group, and in the services provided to my family from the Les Turner ALS Foundation.

In a few short weeks we will head back to New Jersey for our second marathon and we are not nearly as close to our goal as last year, yet every month there are more families coming to the support groups for help! Please share our story with your Facebook friends and family members. I'm typing this blog because I am fortunate enough to have technology that allows me to communicate with you even though I have lost my speech and the use of my arms and hands. Help us provide this and other needed equipment and services to others living with ALS! Click the link above to connect to our website and help or share my blog through Facebook.

Please don't let this opportunity pass; someone is diagnosed with this disease every ninety minutes, help us stop it!

Thank you, dd".

CHAPTER 3

The Love Story of a Family

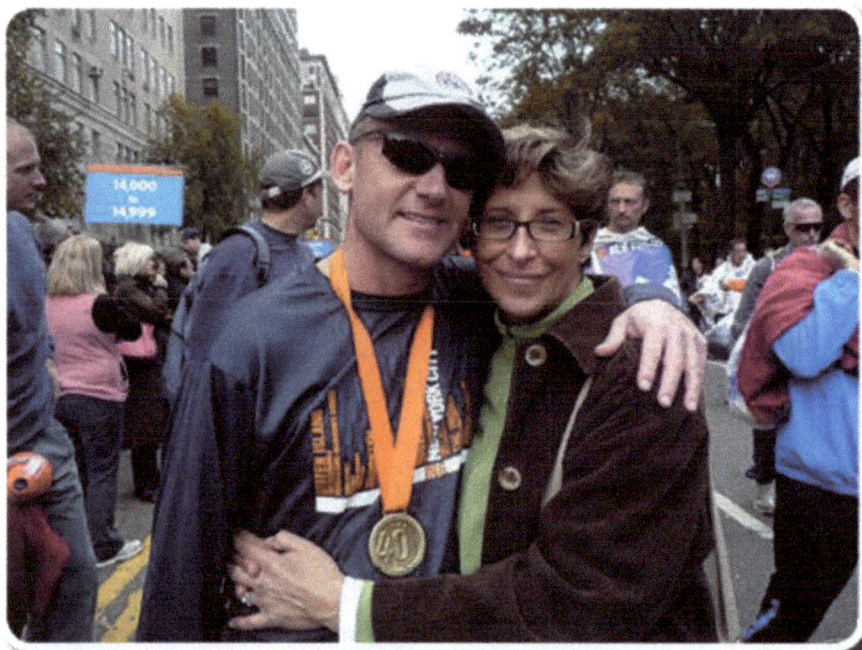

Finish of the New York City Marathon 2009. Just 2 days ago I asked Denise to marry me and she said YES!!

In the fall of 2009, I met a girl. Not in the traditional way-I met

Denise via eHarmony. Yes, we were a Harmony success story. We often joked about the Harmony commercials with the two incredibly good-looking people dancing in a beautiful garden or around a fountain. We thought how cool it would be for us to be featured in a commercial, dancing around with our wheelchair. (I'm not sure why we never got that call. One of the world's unsolved mysteries.)

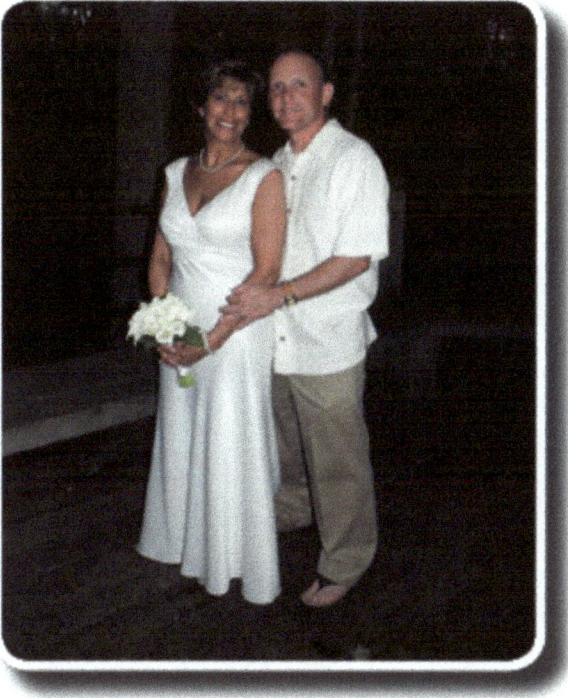

Our wedding June 18, 2010.

She makes me cuter than 1 am.

Denise was unlike anyone I'd ever met. She was beautiful, smart, and had a soul that was unmatched. When I met her, I was in a very dark place. She was the light that got me through the dark place. She would talk to me for hours, either face to face, on a long walk through a forest preserve, or on the phone. She never cast judgment, and she built me up. I knew this woman was living life as God intended and always putting others ahead of herself. I'd never experienced that before. She always put her faith first and figured everything would fall into place.

After several years of being divorced, I found myself in a relationship that was obviously unhealthy. I refused to see some of the signs, but as I look back, I realize I wasn't seeing anything clearly. I had good times and bad times and many counseling sessions about it. During one of those counseling sessions my gifted therapist came straight out and said, "Chris, you are in a dysfunctional relationship." Those words rang true and that relationship ended thereafter. (Thank you, Jamie, for showing me the light!)

As it turned out, that was a blessing in disguise, because along came Denise.

She and I both were playing around with several dating sites with no luck, so we tried Harmony, hoping that it would be a bit more real. We both had some bad/awkward dates on other sites and friends told us about the Christian part of eHarmony. We were perplexed and gave it a shot.

Having a drink together on a warm summer day. I
loved those times together. I love this woman.

She had the strongest faith of anyone I ever met. I, not so much,
but a good friend convinced me to give it a shot. Both Denise and
I never had any other matches than each other. We had others but
we only contacted each other. It was a long process with all the
question submitting and answering. It was so tiring but so worth
it when we were finally permitted to talk to each other by phone.
She had a highly stressful job at Schwarz Supply Source and she
was alone raising her daughter, so we never talked until around
9:00 at night. And boy did we talk.

We literally talked for hours, and then at 2:00 a.m. we'd realize we
needed to get to bed. This happened so often. We talked about
everything under the sun. We knew each other so well by the time
we had our first date at Chili's. I was a nervous wreck and almost
tossed the flowers I had gotten her in the garbage because I didn't

want to be over the top. She loved them and it was like we knew each other already.

She was kind of sad because her company was having cutbacks and she had to let go of someone she really liked. It was so hard for her. She showed me his response on her Blackberry and I knew there was something so special about her.

The guy she let go sent the nicest e-mail to her and I knew this was someone I needed because she made me better than I was. We had a long dinner and shared fajitas for two.

We hugged when it was over but neither one of us wanted to let go. I was like a school kid in love with the prom queen. We continued to see each other whenever we could. We went on long walks through the forest preserve, bike riding, rollerblading (she was so fast!), cross-country skiing, and so much more. We were the perfect match. Thank you, eHarmony.

Suffice it to say: Denise saved me from myself. She gave me my faith back and even persuaded me to get baptized a few years back. She was my rock and I owe her my life.

On a side note, the first time I got enough courage to kiss her I was so taken by her. I remember thanking her for not slapping me after I kissed her. She just smiled. She had the greatest smile ever. I can still see that smile and am still amazed. Her smile has been described as "infectious" —that was so true! She could light up any room she entered by flashing that flawless smile.

That smile was one of many facets of Denise's life that pulled from the shadows of a tough divorce. I got divorced when my daughter Leah was in kindergarten. It was so awful. I've certainly taken ownership for my part in the whole debacle. The bottom line is we were too young to get married (early twenties is way too early).

Divorce with a child involved did not suit me at all. I hated the whole

"Alternate weekend's visitation here" and holidays. It wasn't fair to Leah. We made it work but I still carry guilt over it all. Fortunately, my ex and I have a great relationship. Thank God for that. She and her parents actually went to Denise's Celebration of Life on September 18, 2016.

Denise also had a child from a previous marriage. Her name was Maddie and she was adopted from China at the age of about six months. She was absolutely everything Denise wanted in a daughter. She was outgoing, smart, funny, and loved acting, singing, and the theater. Denise spent every minute making her daughter the best she could be. No one loved her daughter like Denise did.

Maddie had some rough spots as she went through life, but one of them was not her mom being sick. Yes, it influenced her, but Denise never gave her the opportunity to use it as a crutch or excuse. She parented as if she had 100 percent mobility. Maddie was cared for, loved, and valued. What else would a daughter want? Denise's parented with grace and beauty.

All the challenges that faced Denise did not stop Maddie from experiencing everything a child should. She was the love of Denise's life. She loved her with everything she had. One thing that Denise did for Maddie that was off-the-charts awesome was to have faith and believe. This was instilled at an early age and it grew in Maddie, so much so that a couple of years ago Maddie decided to get baptized. This was such a momentous occasion for Maddie as well as Denise. In a time when Denise could have turned her back on her faith, she leaned into it and gave a great gift to her daughter. This is one example of how Denise was so impactful.

Maddie is now thirteen and living in Brooklyn with her dad. She was the most important person in Denise's life and was everything she wanted her to be. I had the privilege of living with her for about seven years. It makes me sad that I don't see Maddie much anymore and I pray she is having the time of her life with her dad and stepmom. I look forward to her occasional texts, and hopefully I will see her again someday. In some ways it's good that Maddie lives far from Illinois.

She had a rough year last year and moving to Brooklyn gave her a new start. I know she will go far in life, if given the opportunity. Her mom prepared her for a very successful faith-filled life.

As for my daughter, Leah, she met Denise when she was in the eighth grade.

They, too, had a bond that formed quickly with real strength. Before their first meeting, Denise mentioned to me how nervous she was to meet Leah. I relayed this to my ex, Tracy, and she counseled Denise to just be herself and Leah would love her. And she did.

Leah's High School Graduation Party.

I love this family picture.

Those two hit it off perfectly, as they shared a passion for the theater. Leah had just started her acting career and Denise and she talked and talked. It was beautiful to behold. The two people I loved more than anything were two peas in a pod.

This relationship grew as Leah spent more time with Denise. Their remarkable connection grew, and Denise loved her like she was her own. On a side note, they often ganged up on me to give me a hard time, but I loved every minute of it. It was Denise who told Leah about following her passion in life. Denise also showed up at all of Leah's plays and went to every school dance. There, Leah always made sure she could get a picture just with Denise. It almost made me cry each time, but then again, I am a big baby.

Once we were at a Chris Tomlin concert at Willow Creek Church, but Leah was getting fitted for her prom dress. Leah tweeted @ Chris Tomlin and he proceeded to give Denise a shout-out and pray over her. A friend captured this incredible moment on video. This was yet another example of Leah's love for Denise.

I'd be remiss if I didn't thank Tracy for the advice, she gave Denise early on: to simply be herself and Denise would be drawn to her. It meant so much to us.

One of my proudest moments was at Denise's "Celebration of Life," when Leah got up and talked so emotionally about Denise. She chose a song to play for Denise called "Miss You." All that Leah had to say deeply reinforced in me how Denise was a direct blessing from the God. I don't know why the ALS had to be part of it, but someday it will be revealed, I'm sure.

Leah is now nineteen and a sophomore at Southern Illinois University in Edwardsville, studying elementary education. She still loves the theater, a passion all three girls shared. I know Leah misses Denise a lot; I could tell when she spoke at Denise's "Celebration of Life."

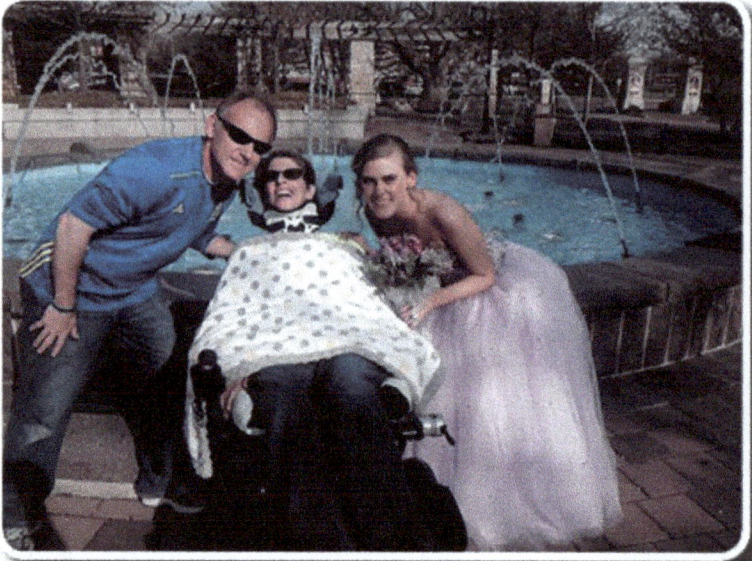

This is Leah's Sr. Prom. Denise went to pictures at all of Leah's dances. Leah always made sure to get a picture with Denise.

What is important to note again is the depth and breadth of Denise's faith.

This faith in Jesus allowed her to fight this disease more every day. I know in the end that ALS won, but I still say she spent five-plus years kicking its butt. It truly is staggering what faith can do for a person if you just trust it. That is a trait that I hope I can have one day.

In addition to having wonderful people entering our orbit, we clung to each other throughout Denise's battle. She discussed one memorable night when we thought we'd "escape reality" and head to the movies, but instead ended up bawling our eyes out and literally clinging to each other. Unless you've walked through a deep, dark valley with your spouse, you can't imagine the closeness that it produces in your relationship. Sure, many couples divorce when one partner receives a dire diagnosis, but those that stay together will all tell you that their relationship deepened to an entirely new level, an unimaginable level of intimacy.

That was surely true for Denise and me.

Here is her review of the film Love & Other Drugs, along with a description of our night out at the movies.

"Shortly after learning that the Neurology Team at the Mayo Clinic could not find any evidence contrary to our original diagnosis, we decided to take a break from reality and head for the local movie theater. We needed to stay another night for the appointments scheduled the next day before we could travel home, so it seemed like a good distraction.

We looked at the listings on my Blackberry and remembered we had seen a trailer for a romantic comedy called "Love and Other Drugs," with Anne Hathaway and Jake Gyllenhaal, and decided it was just what we needed to escape for a short time.

Ironically, when we originally saw the trailer, we must have missed the part that set you up for the underlying story line in which Maggie, the lead character played by Anne Hathaway, was struggling with the early stages of Parkinson's disease.

I'm certain that for a typical couple it was an entertaining film. It could undoubtedly be classified as a chick flick, but the men in the audience were treated to seeing plenty of Anne Hathaway, while the women were likely agonizing over the sad love story. Nonetheless, for us, in the midst of dealing with our own situation, this was anything but an escape from our reality.

In the end Jamie, played by Jake Gyllenhaal, decides that Parkinson's

Disease or not, he loved Maggie and he wasn't going to walk away... we held each other and wept through the movie.

Nearly a year later, I can tell you that this disease has not torn us apart. If anything, I believe it has made us closer, and our commitment stronger. That's not to say it doesn't challenge us most days; it does... but with humor, grace, and love, my husband, Chris, gets me through each day..."

I'm so honored that Denise wrote about me in that way, but to be honest, I'm not sure who helped whom get through each day. I am sure that some days it was the other way around.

Denise wasn't done praising me (much to my embarrassment), but I share the following post as well to help you understand our iron-strong relationship and boundless love for each other. It's true: I haven't traditionally seen myself as a leader. Perhaps you don't see yourself as one, either. But, as Denise describes, there might be a hidden leader in you, especially if you step out and begin to help others. Chew on this post for a while, and may it make a difference in your life and the lives of those you will benefit.

Enjoy "The Art of Possibilities" from February 4, 2012:

"I have always enjoyed learning as an adult, and in particular I enjoy any form of learning related to leadership. I've been fortunate to have had the opportunity to attend business conferences and leadership conferences, to hear many of my favorite authors, motivational speakers, and leaders from a vast array of industries and professions teach. I'm sure my former co-workers are chuckling at the idea that I may have read yet another book that I'm all excited about sharing with them...

In the summer of 2009, I invited my husband Chris to attend one such leadership conference and I was surprised by his response that went something like this: 'T'm not a leader, I'm a follower.' Wow! I thought, you get up in front of groups of children all day long and teach, and you don't see yourself as a leader? This boggled my mind, and I still wonder if there are others like him who feel the same way.

More than a decade ago, I read a book titled The Art of Possibilities written by Rosamund Stone Zander, family therapist, and her husband, Benjamin Zander, conductor of the Boston Philharmonic Orchestra and teacher at the New England Conservatory of Music. Their diverse experiences gave shape to interesting perspectives on leadership and it remains one of my favorite books to this day.

Benjamin talked about a few ideas that helped to shape my thinking as a leader over the years. One was 'Giving an A in the Workplace. This idea reminded me that everyone has something to contribute, and my job as a leader was to create an environment in which people were appropriately tasked with responsibilities that allowed them to feel valued for what they had to offer. It also meant I had to give them the benefit of believing that they wanted earn an 'A,' and examine the situation if the individual was not appropriately placed and needed reassignment.

The second was his practice of giving his students an 'A' at the beginning of a class but asking then to define in writing exactly how they were going to earn it. This idea was simple to apply in the business environment by getting people involved in their goal setting, shaping their roles in the organization, asking them what they enjoyed doing, and what they wanted to achieve. This approach increased ownership and helped to open our minds to tackling more challenging business issues.

The third idea that really resonated with me was: 'Leading from Any Chair.' This, in short, means you don't have to be the conductor to lead the orchestra, or in the business environment, you don't have to be the CEO, the owner, or even the boss to lead change, something I always felt passionate about. If what you want to do makes sense, no one will stop you from taking it on, and they may even decide to jump in and help you get it done!

How does this apply to my 'Adventures in Losing Stability'? When I think about how Taylor and Delaney approached the idea of devoting their community service project to create an event that would help raise awareness and funds, to support research and patient care for those suffering from ALS, I could not help but see these young women as future leaders.

The written outline of their plan detailed each activity, expense, and expected proceeds to reach their goal of $5000, and they thought of everything! No one told these girls they couldn't do it, and they took off with a running start. They recruited family, friends, parents, teachers and even secured business sponsors to participate; it was truly a successful community event, and they have already started talking about how to make it even better next year!

Near the end of the event, I had the pleasure of meeting the girl's Social Studies teacher and mentor, Mr. Bakke. Shortly after, another teacher pointed him out and whispered in my ear 'That's their teacher. I've heard him speak and he's a really awesome teacher!' I don't doubt that...

I also met the girls' families: Lisa Gibbons and Jennifer Morrissey, siblings, aunts, and grandparents who were all fully engaged in making the event a huge success.

So, as I sit here writing this, I wonder...does Mr. Bakke think of himself as a leader?

Do these parents see themselves as leaders? And do they see

these two bright young women as examples of the leaders that will emerge from their generation?

And finally, does Chris see himself as a leader, recognizing that this all started because he took the lead, setting a challenging goal to push me for 26.2 miles, and inspired two young women, and a community he served for 23 years, to get behind him in support of reaching it?

From where I'm sitting... I surely do."

CHAPTER 4

Faith

I probably haven't talked enough about the role of Denise's Christian faith in all of this. I'm not the type of person to hit people over the head with my personal beliefs, but to omit Denise's walk with God would be erroneous and inaccurate.

The fact is she had a vibrant faith in God, a very sacred daily walk with Him.

During her years of decline physically, she actually grew astronomically in the spiritual area, as so often happens in cases like hers. God uses many ways to draw us closer to Himself. In Denise's case, he used ALS to draw both of us nearer to Him. In that regard, I am thankful for ALS, as odd as that may sound. I have a new rock-solid faith that Denise demonstrated for me day after day.

Denise's baptism in the lake at Willow Creek. Her
faith and belief in God were unmatched.

In this post Denise commented on one of the many Christian books
that she devoured in her spare time. She entitled it "Choosing to
See," after the book sharing the same title.

"Last year I read the book Choosing to See, written by Mary Beth
Chapman, the wife of a well-known Christian artist, Steven Curtis
Chapman. In it she writes about her journey through the grieving
process after the accidental death of their 5-year-old daughter,
Maria Sue.

Something about the title and description drew me in. The loss of a child remains to be the most traumatic experience I could ever imagine having to endure. I lost a younger sibling at the age of 23, and to this day I cannot think of any other event that had a greater impact on me and my family. Even now, when I am forced to face the reality of my own mortality, it doesn't come close to the overwhelming grief I experienced at that time.

I had previously purchased a copy of "Beauty Will Rise," the CD that Steven Curtis Chapman released after the loss of Maria Sue. This collection of songs was by far the best of his work I had yet to hear. I remember thinking how the lyrics were filled with the pain I had experienced as I moved in and out of the emotional stages of grief, and yet they managed to come through the experience transformed by faith and hope. I purchased several copies that year to give as gifts, thinking no matter the reason for grieving, in the end, the process was the same and these words could heal people.

I am still impressed by this couple and their courage to share their journey with us, no matter how personal and painful the experience has been, and although at the time I had no idea of the journey that was unfolding before me, through them I have been inspired to see God's hand in my own journey.

'Choosing to see' for me means not to become angry with God for allowing this disease to take my life as I knew it, but instead finding the many ways in which we are blessed by these changes, and blessed by those who have joined us on this journey.

I have always joked that my glass is not half empty or even half full. My glass is overflowing, and that has remained unchanged even through this challenge.

My faith simply will not allow it!"

Okay, time-out here. I've got to get rid of this huge lump in my throat as I reread these words. Denise's glass "overflowing?" Are you kidding me?! This woman set an example for anyone dealing with major hardship. She inspired those of us who were around her for years, and I hope this book will encourage thousands upon thousands as well, long outliving her physical life on Earth.

I think part of my motivation for writing is to have a sliver of the impact that couples like the Chapmans have had. Their walk through the dark forest of deep pain did so much to give Denise perspective, and she inevitably passed a lot of that perspective onto me.

One of the things that attracted me to Denise was the aura around her. As long as I knew her, she was always putting others first and herself a distant second.

Her soul was unmatched and she thoroughly enjoyed following Jesus first, with everything else coming second. I often wondered how she was able to remain positive while being engaged in the fight of her life.

Just last summer, the Fourth of July to be exact, we were watching a movie called Miracles from Heaven, a powerful flick about faith and trust in God. As I wondered how Denise could stay so upbeat throughout her ordeal, I had an insight via a quote from Albert Einstein that was used in the movie: "There are two ways to live your life. As if NOTHING is a miracle or as if EVERYTHING is a miracle." The reason Denise was able to live so well as ALS stole everything from her was because, to her, everything was a miracle. Her incredible faith in God no doubt played a part in this approach to life.

Imagine if, starting today, we all lived life as if everything was a miracle. How much better would this world be? If Denise could do it, given all she had to deal with, I'm sure we all could as well.

My spiritual background prepared me to go deeper with Denise but did not produce the kind of depth that she had when we met. I was raised Catholic and went to Catholic school from first to twelfth grade. I never really connected to the church and it was not a key part of my life for a long time-until I met Denise.

Within a week of seeing her, I asked if she would take me to her church. She did and I was quickly back on the road as a follower, not a wanderer.

When Denise got sick, I found myself praying, reading the Bible and attending church regularly with Denise. It was so good for my soul! One day Denise asked me if I would get baptized before she passed away. As a result, on a warm Sunday in June I gave my life to Jesus and was baptized. That was a game changer for me and Denise was thrilled. She had a colossal impact on my life in the spiritual realm. If you had told me that I'd get baptized at age forty-six, I would have laughed.

As I write, I will honestly confess that at this moment, my faith is being sorely tested. I don't understand why Denise was taken from me after I had spent such a small amount of time with her. Why did she have to be in so much pain? What is the Master Plan? Will it ever be revealed? These are the questions I grapple with as I try to make sense of my journey to this point. Perhaps you have tussled with them too.

My questions, which continue to rattle around in my head even after Denise's passing, were matched by at least as many in Denise's mind as she did battle with ALS. She gave insight into the cycle of questions and answers as we interacted with medical professionals over several years' time in a blog post titled: "Still Searching for Answers."

"The summer was moving fast and we were still searching for

something that could explain my dragging right leg, loss of balance, and the random twitching of fingers on my right hand, which by the way only seemed to happen in the still of the night.

I also noticed about the same time that my fingers were weakening, and it became difficult to write in the same block printing style I'd come to recognize as my own handwriting.

At first, I considered the change to be a symptom of a cultural shift from using pen and paper, to typing e-mails and texting on my Blackberry. How often did I actually write anymore? I remember asking my coworkers if they were noticing the same thing, but no one seemed to be jumping on my cultural shift theory.

The orthopedist ordered a series of blood tests, x-rays, and MRIs in July, and referred me to a neurologist. I'd had my fair share of blood tests and x-rays, but the MRI would be a new experience. I learned this procedure was fairly uneventful; although you must lay completely still, with ear plugs, if you're lucky enough to be offered them, and you pray that you don't get the sudden urge to scratch your nose, which inevitably will drive you nuts for the next 45 minutes!

The doctor actually ordered several of these MRI's to be performed, and I learned that sometimes the procedure was done on the same area of the body twice, once in the standard fashion, and then a second time using a dye that was set up intravenously. I was not crazy about this added amenity. The complimentary ear plugs were enough, but this particular sequence of imaging was going to be of my brain, and the technician did not resemble Nurse Ratched, so I complied. Frankly, you could easily gain consensus that it was about time I had my head examined anyway.

So now we've got the dye set up, and we're ready for brain imaging in technicolor, and over and over the technician warns me that if

I move, we'll have to start the whole process all over again, so at this point the best I could hope for was that I could manage to relax, and maybe fall asleep. After all, who wouldn't want to enjoy a midday siesta? Thankfully, I slept through most of these tests and emerged from the cocoon-like contraption virtually unscathed and well rested.

Spinal taps were an entirely different experience..."

As you read about another difficult step in Denise's journey, let me ask you a question: How many times did you smile while reading the post above? See what I mean about this woman's spirit, how she somehow picked up your mood as she wrote about what has proven to be a terrifying experience for many? This gives you a little idea of what it was like to be around her every day. There's a certain type of person who, when suffering, somehow lifts the spirits of those who come to console him or her. We all have had those types of people in our lives, the ones we visit in the hospital who elevate our mood despite their suffering. That was Denise. That was my wife. You can see why I call myself "blessed" to have spent as long as I did with her.

Denise's questions weren't limited to accurate diagnoses. She also wrestled with God's purpose in her predicament, a struggle many of us shared-and still battle. In a fair number of her blog posts, Denise touched on the many confusing thoughts that a serious disease can produce. This is part of the struggle that I think a lot of people miss; they see the outward, physical challenges but often don't think of the inward, mental gymnastics that occur every day in the minds of the afflicted.

Denise thought a lot about Maddie's future, even as she contemplated her own thoughts as she watched her mother decline in a similar fashion, also leaving this Earth far too soon. In

"Parallel Lives," Denise highlighted some of the eerie similarities between her journey and Maddie's.

"There is a belief in China that when a child is born, an 'invisible red thread' connects the child's soul to all the people: past, present and future, who will play a part in that child's life. If you subscribe to this belief, it was simply destiny that my Chinese-born daughter is beside me on this journey.

Initially, upon learning of my diagnosis, I was devastated by the thought that she would have to witness my eventual decline and lose her mom much sooner than seemed fair. The question of why.... why would God have joined us only to bring such pain and grief to a child? I have no answer to that question, only deep sorrow surrounding the reality of it.

Although she and I do not share any biological connection, there are so many ways in which I see myself in her. I guess it has always been a question of nature vs. nurture, but there is a connection between us that I've always felt but never expected would play out in this way.

I remember the day vividly in my mind's eye; it was my eighth birthday, I was sitting on a bench in front of the five-story apartment building we lived in, waiting for my parents. In my hands was a brand-new red transistor radio, a gift I received that very day. While my attention was clearly on my new toy, I do recall my thoughts as I noticed my parents walking out of the building. It's likely that this was not something new I'd seen, but for the first time my usually self-centered focus turned toward them and processed what was happening. Why did my mom need to hold onto my dad's arm so tightly? Why couldn't she walk on her own?

Was someone going to explain this to me?

She was diagnosed right after I was born; it was neurological, and by the time my eight-year-old brain noticed, it looked a lot like what I am currently emulating today. It was not ALS, but there were a lot of symptomatic similarities that played out in a gradual progression of decline that a child could miss. Sadly, we lost her when I was just 16 years old. My daughter recently began to ask how old my mom was when she died, and I dance around the subject because I cannot bring myself to tell her that she was the very same age I am today.

So, here I sit with both the perspective of a mom frustrated by the reality of her physical limitations and the memory of what it was like to be eight and realize my mom was different, but not in a good way...

I've been told that my story is uniquely my own; it is not my mom's story or my daughter's story, and that my experience as a child provides an awareness my mom didn't have. I pray that awareness evokes wisdom, patience and understanding as we travel this path together; I would not have chosen this for her..."

And now for the real confusing part, the multiplication of questions without good answers, the misreading of signs, from rainbows to veteran practitioners, the hope that springs inside all of us as Christmas approaches. We held out as best we could, praying for a miracle, a miracle that didn't come. Denise wrote poignantly about this time in "Holding out Hope."

"It was late December 2010, Christmas was only five days away, and we found ourselves sitting in a tiny room at the Mayo Clinic in Rochester, Minnesota, under 38 inches of reported snowfall, getting a second opinion...holding out hope that the young neurologist we saw at home was wrong about the diagnosis.

I prayed over and over on the long drive out, that God would intervene and we would get better news. Upon arrival at the exit for Rochester, I saw a rainbow in the sky and wanted to believe it was a sign of hope.

After all, the doctor couldn't be more than twelve; he must have missed something... I was served a death sentence, and I wasn't going to accept it from someone who had the ringtone on his iPhone configured to quack like a duck.

Funny, yes... and being the geek that I am, I could appreciate the humor, but also being a child of the sixties, I needed someone like Marcus Welby, M.D., to check things out.

The Mayo Clinic is an amazing place. Within minutes of our initial meeting, we had a four-day schedule of appointments with specialist and tests to be performed. This included: the collecting of all of the compulsory body fluids for testing, a pulmonary test, another spinal tap and another EMG!

Bravo to the delightful woman who performed the spinal tap without consequence.

She stood less than five feet tall and likely weighed in at less than 100 lbs. She spent a few minutes introducing herself and explaining what she was going to do as I would lay on my side, facing the wall. No need to remove my clothing or even my shoes, she simply said, it works best when we just chat during the procedure. So, we talked about our kids, as moms often do, and in a small exam room without a fancy gravity table, x-ray machine or team of medical professionals, she got the job done!

Never underestimate the gentle finesse of a woman.

The EMG, however, was equally as painful as the first one, but necessary I suppose, and the pulmonary tests were interesting. I had a cast from a broken wrist that reached up my arm nearly to my shoulder, making it difficult to use the arm for anything, so they had to call in a lip holder to assist in the testing. This was a tad awkward for both the designated lip holder and me; it's best you don't try to visualize it.

Organized, efficient and thorough, the Mayo team reached a conclusion in three days that had taken our doctors at home the better part of the last nine months to determine. Unfortunately, our Doogie Howser was right, and after we met with the specialist who delivered the confirmation, we sat with a nurse who was charged with the task of educating us on what to be prepared for as the disease progressed, clearly not the fun part of her day.

I remember taking some notes with my pad and pen, hardly legible as my tears were hitting the page, making the ink run. I'm sure I still have those notes, and the folder filled with resource information that would lay untouched for months after we returned home. It was only a couple of weeks since the first diagnosis and the confirmation stung, throwing us both back into a state of shock.

We had the answers we had come for but it was a long, quiet drive home..."

To say our ride home from the Mayo Clinic was tough would be the biggest understatement ever. You've just received the deadly diagnosis of ALS and a death sentence. What do you do? Where do you turn? I was so angry at God for this situation with my wife of only about five months. Our world was shattered. At least mine was. Denise, on the other hand, turned to her faith. I remember driving and her saying, "You know God didn't give me ALS. He must have some sort of plan for us. Let's pray about that and maybe we will get some answers."

Really? You've just been handed a death sentence and you want to pray about it?! I didn't verbalize that, as it would have done no one any good. So, for about fifteen to twenty minutes of our drive we sat in silence and prayed. I won't share my prayer because there may be kids reading this. Suffice to say, it wasn't a nice prayer. It was more of me giving God a piece of my mind. They say it's okay to let God know when you're mad. I hope so, because if it's not I might have just punched my ticket to a place that is a tad bit warmer than I would like.

In contrast, Denise seemed to be calmed by this simple gesture of asking God for answers. She seemed to be enveloped by a warmth and a calm I couldn't fathom. I believe on that day Denise had an actual conversation with God and was told that she had a whole lot more to do here on Earth before the end. It was that passion that enabled her to spend the rest of her time on Earth helping others. She blessed so many others in the five-plus years battling this disease. It's hard to put into words, but I have a quote from a man that was touched by Denise a very short time after meeting her.

His name was Mike and he was the guy who helped build a running chair for Denise. He worked for Dick Hoyt Racing in Boston. The chair was built because her other chair was giving her all kinds of pain, so he decided to make a new one, which we used in Boston in 2016, our last race together.

Mike has a mission statement that he tries to adhere to every day: "My great aim is to love others without others loving me in return." He said after meeting Denise that he realized she, too, was living his mission statement. That was Denise in a nutshell: God-loving, faith-filled, and always putting others first.

So, on that car ride home from Mayo I realized that we weren't done. We were only just starting. God had plans. Big plans for Denise and me.

Denise had always seen our coming together as part of God's

master plan, a view that I, of course, share. She also saw God's hand in other ways in her life, from losing loved ones early-which taught her to savor each day-to meeting me seemingly by chance. This post, called "God is Always Working Upstream," gives another peek into Denise's spiritual life and how she drew daily sustenance not just from me, but from God.

"I don't remember the first time I heard this phrase ("God is always working upstream.'). I suppose it was at a time in my life when things weren't quite going the way I wanted, and someone gently tossed it out in hopes that I could grab onto it and believe that it was all for the best. While at the time I doubt it felt like anything more than a Band-aid on a gushing open wound, it was recorded somewhere in my psyche, so one day it could be summoned after the bleeding ceased. Many years later, I stand firmly on this belief.

It has also been said that if you stand too close to a mural, you can only see splashes of color, but as you distance yourself from it, the image comes into focus; herein lays the problem. We make our decisions based on our particular perspective at any given moment in time, without the benefit of knowing what's ahead of us. As Julia Sweeney says, 'We make plans and God says, "Ha!"'

So, it seems, that even as a self-proclaimed pragmatist, I've taken some wrong turns and made some poor choices; I've also had my fair share of events outside of my control which wreak havoc in my life. But with distance, and reflection, I began to see the safety nets, which were carefully placed around me, before I ever realized I needed them... and how some of these events shaped the woman I've become.

Therefore, had I not had the experience of losing my mom, my younger brother and my dad, each independently before I reached the age of thirty, I might not have realized how fragile life is, and I might not have pushed myself so hard, and I might not have taken the risks that made my life so rich.

I met my husband, Chris, about a year before my first symptoms appeared, and we were married just shy of 6 months before my diagnosis. Who could have ever imagined that our commitment for better or for worse, in sickness and in health, would be tested so soon?

These days I tend to dwell in Joshua 1:9: 'Have I not commanded you? Be strong and courageous. Do not be afraid; do not be discouraged, for the LORD your God will be with you wherever you go, because I can see the foundation of support around me, and I can trust that He is still ahead of me preparing the way... Chris standing beside me is all the proof I need."

That, my friends, is the definition of faith.

Another aspect of life where I think Denise's faith made a huge difference was in the area of pain. So many people that struggle with constant pain give in to the sweet serenade of opioids. Others succumb to the psychological weight of their suffering and can hardly live without a steady diet of antidepressants. Denise wrote about these temptations as she gave tips on pill organization in her trademark humorous way. In a blog post titled "The Domino Effect," she wrote:

"There is no cure for ALS yet, but there are medications your doctor can prescribe for the symptoms. For me it's been anti-inflammatory drugs to reduce pain and muscle relaxers to try to relieve some of the spasticity. Most of these medications come with their own set of adverse side effects. No worries though, they can also prescribe medication for the side effects...And so begins the domino effect, but where does it end?

Before you know it your head is spinning and it takes an hour once a week just to fill those tiny compartments in your day-of-the-week pill organizer! Oh yes, you'll need one of those; try to avoid the ones that look like a mid-size tackle box. They have the a.m., mid-day, evening and bedtime compartments for each day; helpful to those who need to take different medications multiple times a day.

However, I would suggest you exercise caution. If you would consider yourself to be someone akin to Felix Unger, it's tempting to get the tackle box and be that organized, but wait until you need to get those tiny pills out of the mid-day Wednesday slot! Not so easy with the loss of fine motor skills in your fingers.

I recommend the single compartment, day-of-the-week organizer with the locking lids. Get more than one if you need an a.m., p.m., etc. You can just open the lid for Wednesday, and pour those little buggers into your hand or a dixie cup.

If you're more of an Oscar Madison type, with any luck you're married to a Felix type and it's already been taken care of for you... and its color coded, not that you care... but try to make it seem like you do.

All that said...you really need to decide for yourself how you want to handle all the prescriptions they hand you before it gets out of control. It's sort of like doing a cost/benefit analysis, only you have to weigh the benefit against the discomfort, and you have choices.

In my experience, some muscle relaxers can cause some of the necessary muscles to lose control, not so good if it affects the plumbing. Now, they can fix that with another medication, but this one could cause a backup on the other end, so you'll want to give it some serious consideration.

Or, you can take the one that causes acid reflux, but Pepcid

Complete should take care of that, and if not, we can get you a prescription for Nexium, the little purple pill, you've likely seen the commercial for that one.

There is another option, but it can cause your legs to feel rubbery and unstable, so start with a smaller dosage and increase gradually. So, you give it a try and okay, things are going well, no rubber legs but... well, if you admit that you're feeling a little sad and you find yourself crying over the silly things like feeling pressured to decide what to have for dinner, that statement will earn you a prescription for an antidepressant faster than you can say Zoloft!

No thanks, my pill organizer is full.

There's no room for Zoloft.

You've got to draw the line somewhere..."

Another aspect of Denise's faith that I always appreciated-and still appreciate-was her very honest struggle with her attitude and desire to please God in all things as her body functioned to a lesser and lesser degree. I don't think any of us can understand what it's like to have ALS unless this horrible malady has actually invaded our own bodies. Denise gives great insight into what an ALS patient thinks and feels around holiday time, a time when Denise knew that she should count her blessings, but began to be resigned to the inexorable march of ALS. Enter her struggle in this 2011 post entitled "Thanksgiving."

"First, I feel that I must preface this post with an explanation, as I am getting phone calls, e-mails and general inquiries about my condition. Since we have had a bit of a cold snap, and my allergy trauma should be toned down by now, it seems that the closest of friends are beginning to wonder if I might actually be slacking off at this point... fair enough!

Thank you for your concern. I am getting some relief from the allergy attacks and I have backed off the allergy meds to clear my head. So, I am somewhat functional at this point. However, the title for this post, 'Thanksgiving,' should give you some indication of just how long ago I began working on it.

So... clearly, I am late to the party, but let's just embrace the fact that I've shown up at all and move on to the topic at hand because it is already December, and I am going to end up distracted with my holiday shopping if I sit at this PC much longer.

(Yes, self-diagnosed A.D.D. too...I'm a real prize!)

When I began this post, I really did have Thanksgiving in mind, but as you read it, you may detect the places where interruptions demanded I attend to something else, and well... upon my return, my original train derailed and I ended up on a different track altogether.

In the end, I may have gotten to a different place, but it must have been where I needed to go. After all, this is mostly therapeutic for me, and you are along for the ride...

End of preface.

There are so many things to be thankful for as I reflect on the expanse in my rear view... I have always had all that I needed and then some... and as I grew older and more socially aware, I realized that many of us live in unbelievable excess, while others live in extreme poverty. This concern especially breaks my heart when I see how poverty affects children, so for some time now I have committed time and resources to organizations focused on this issue.

While I have had this awareness of excess for several years now and made some changes in my behavior, if I take an honest inventory, I would have to admit that in my lifetime, I have accumulated much more stuff than I could possibly ever need.

One could easily point to my collection of shoes as empirical evidence of my excessive consumerism. Mind you, that while I am not asking you to let me off the hook, I am not alone in this sin. Many of you are right beside me and you know who you are...

This issue of excess vs. the under-resourced was even more apparent to me after I became sick. In the initial months following my diagnosis, I became obsessed with concern for what to do with all my stuff! I know how crazy that sounds, but it became a pressing issue in my mind, and while the average prognosis gave me 2-5 years to deal with this, my dysfunctional coping mechanism wanted it addressed immediately, if not sooner!

I began to lose weight, so I had a lot of clothes that didn't fit, and months before I had to give up wearing heels, so there were dozens and dozens of pairs of shoes, sandals and boots I could no longer wear, and that was just the tip of the iceberg...

There are accessories, too, and what about my bike, skates, skis, and eventually my car? You can't take it with you, and I was obsessed with giving it away! 'It' being anything I could no longer use.

What was it that drove me to this urgent need to dispense of these material possessions? I remember thinking that I needed to give these things to people who needed them now, and not wait for the time to come when my family would be burdened with the task of going through all of it. I've been there before and it's draining both physically and emotionally. I could spare them some of that…

What I was not prepared for was the impact the task itself would have on me.

Standing in my closet, holding onto a rack for balance with one hand and grabbing clothing with the other, I struggled physically to maneuver as I filled the bags. And then without warning, my eyes flooded with tears and pain came from so deep in my gut that my mouth hung open, and I could hardly breathe. It wasn't a reluctance to part with my things; it was grief, plain and simple.

This exercise was about letting go… giving up those things that were a part of the life I had and transitioning to the next chapter. I wasn't going back, my legs weren't going to magically start working again, and this was the reality that sent me into hysterics.

I have yet to complete this task. I take it in small bites, because grief is a sneaky little devil, and it hides out waiting for its next opportunity to attack… and I still have plenty for which to be thankful."

Gosh, I love that woman! Able to thank God for His blessings even as she said good-bye to working legs. I'm sure I would not have the same gracious attitude if my legs, which are central to my life and work, stopped functioning. Perhaps that's why I ran eight marathons while pushing Denise, because I was literally running for both of us.

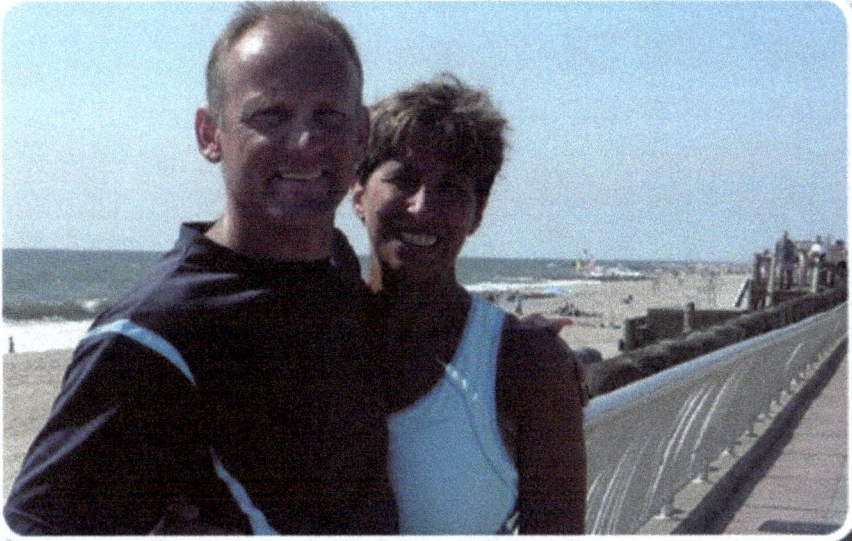

On the boards after running 3 miles. Denise was
so excited. She averaged less than 10 minutes
per mile. 9:46 to be exact. So proud of her.

A few days later Denise again stirred her readers, as she actually gave thanks for her condition while referring to the impactful words of Elizabeth Edwards that she had posted a few days before her death. This post was titled simply "I Believe," and I think it would have made a great alternative title for this book because it summarizes Denise's courageous, head-up perspective throughout living with ALS.

"Have you ever noticed the power Santa garners this time of the year? If you are a parent of young children, I'm pretty sure you do... and I'm guessing you, too, have used it to your advantage.

It seems that magically around Thanksgiving, when all of the stores begin to look like Santa's workshop, children are much more aware of their behavior; they become unusually attentive, obedient and even more affectionate, generously tossing, "I love you Momma," the way they used to toss Cheerios off the tray on their high chairs!

If you haven't seen this change, you have not done your part to foster the myth. Try playing your favorite version of 'Santa Claus Is Comin' To Town' and be sure to sing along loudly. Better yet, encourage them to sing with you, and teach them the lyrics. It seems regardless of age; these clever little humans have the cognitive power to grasp the concept and then...you've got them right where you want them!

Once mastered, it's nearly blissful from mid-November through December!

Now, if for some reason this is not working, and assuming you've done your part, technology can help you. There's a website where you can create a personalized video and send it to your child from Santa. Speaking from experience, this works like a charm! Google PNP (Portable North Pole) Santa and get working on it right away. It's already December 7*™ after all, and you don't have much time left!

By now you're thinking ...Where is she going with this, and how does it relate to ALS?' Well...while thinking about this phenomenon the past few days, and seeing tangible results, my mind wandered off to the premise that we are all children of God, and much like we teach our children about Santa: 'He sees you when you're sleeping, He knows when you're awake, He knows if you've been bad or good, so be good for goodness' sake...' As the lyric goes, many of us are also brought up with the concept that God is all knowing and omnipotent, and one day we will all be accountable for our actions; for some of us... that day will come sooner rather than later.

So, the question is, has that belief impacted my behavior? Sadly, no... I cannot say that knowing this has always influenced my actions, and I can't even say that since learning of my diagnosis, and the inevitable prognosis, I have significantly changed for the better, but my priorities have changed...

December 10, 2010, the morning following news of my diagnosis, I was lying in bed after spending most of the night sleepless, weeping in my husband's arms, and the phone rang. It was early, but looking at the caller ID I could see it was a close friend who knew I would likely be awake, and I was pretty sure she was checking to see how the doctor's appointment went the previous afternoon, so I picked it up.

I'm not sure of what I said, or how she could even understand me with all of the waterworks going on, but I do remember something she shared with me that helped shape my outlook as the dust settled in the months to follow... thank you, my friend.

She told me that Elizabeth Edwards had died just a few days before, on December 7, 2010, and she read me an excerpt from this statement on her Facebook page the day before she passed. I have included the full text below and bolded the excerpt.

You all know that I have been sustained throughout my life by three saving graces

—my family, my friends, and a faith in the power of resilience and hope. These graces have carried me through difficult times and they have brought more joy to the good times than I ever could have imagined. The days of our lives, for all of us, are numbered. We know that. And, yes, there are certainly times when we aren't able to muster as much strength and patience as we would like. It's called being human. But I have found that in the simple act of living with hope, and in the daily effort to have a positive impact in the world, the days I do have are made all the more meaningful and precious. And for that I am grateful. It isn't possible to put into words the love and gratitude I feel to everyone who has and continues to support and inspire me every day. To you I simply say: you know.

With love, Elizabeth

December 6, 2010

Chapel Hill, North Carolina'

Oddly, she died one year ago today as I am writing this, and the excerpt is really all that I can remember from that phone call, but the text is rich with wisdom that has carried me through the past twelve months.

We all know that eventually we will pass, and for those of us who believe in God, we know He's watching, and there will be accountability, but we also know that we are human and fallible and we are forgiven.

So, while I know my time here will end sooner than I had anticipated, I take comfort in the opportunity to spend my remaining time finding ways to savor the moments, to leave nothing unsaid, and love without limits...because in the end, that's all that really matters, and having this time is a blessing because... I believe."

If you didn't gain tremendous perspective from that post, then you need to reread it again. Elizabeth Edwards passed on great wisdom in the days before she died; Denise matched hers, I think, as she wrestled with the same questions and came down on the side of faith. She set a clear-cut example for me, and I pray that she will impact you as well.

The last post in this important chapter will summarize Denise in a nutshell: constant sense of humor, thankfulness in the darkness, struggling to please Godwith her inner thoughts, concluding with a vow to bless others. Join me in admiring this rare woman. Enjoy "It's Been Too Long."

"Several months have passed, the mild winter gave way to a warm spring, a searing hot summer, and this morning I snuggled under the covers as crisp autumn air filled the room. Quite a lot has changed since last winter; I hardly know where to begin...

We landed in a beautiful ranch home on the perimeter of a small suburban subdivision, adjacent to an expanse of farmland that reminds me of growing up in the Garden State. Most days I am at peace as I work within my limitations and surrender worry to hands far bigger and stronger than mine. All that I need has been provided and then some... much more than I could imagine, and much more than I deserve. I realize these are all gifts.

We did not get here on our own; there are countless pairs of hands and feet that carried us. The list of overdues thank-you notes is overwhelming. I have not lost my manners, but my hands betray me. I am so grateful for each of you, you know who you are... Don't give up on me!

We attended a 'voluntary wellness screening last weekend, where they take your vital signs, draw blood, and everyone reports on how many servings of fruits and vegetables they eat a day. In my condition this strikes me as nothing short of humorous. Most of my meals are consumed through a feeding tube. It's been a while since I could honestly describe my exercise routine as cardio, and how do I respond to questions such as, 'How ready are you to make changes in your lifestyle to improve your resistance to germs?' ... Seriously?

Okay, I'll play along, but do they really think these surveys have value? Are they really collecting useful data? I stand firmly on the position that health nuts find it affirming and the rest of us have a skewed perception of what qualifies as a serving of vegetables!

Nonetheless, one question did get me thinking... it went something like this... 'Do you belong to a group or organization where you feel you are making a contribution?' Now we're getting somewhere! Isn't that what makes us thrive? Isn't that what makes us get out of bed in the morning when we could otherwise pull the covers over our heads and go back to sleep? Normally a question like this would get my mind dancing, but on that particular morning, sitting in my wheelchair, it was convicting.

Almost instantly, one of my favorite verses slipped into consciousness: 'For everyone to whom much is given, of him shall much be required. —Luke 12:48 or in The Message translation: ... 'Great gifts mean great responsibilities; greater gifts, greater responsibilities. An immense sense of gratitude washed over me, followed in equal measure by a healthy dose of Catholic guilt, the remains of old programing. Who am I to be so fortunate, and while I sit here consuming resources, how am I making a contribution? How can I make good use of the time and capabilities I have left?

One week has passed since I began writing this post. The process is slow, as I toil daily the typing leads to fatigue, but I press on hoping to find the answer...

Today I conclude with this challenge... Despite the struggle to speak, weakened muscles and uncooperative hands, vow to bless one person a day, to love them, to demonstrate one random act of kindness, and focus on what I can do, not what I cannot..."

CHAPTER 5

The Physical Side

Ultimately, any story about living with ALS has to focus on the physical side of the struggle. That's because ALS attacks the body, although "attacks" is probably too strong of a word. It's more like the proverbial death by a thousand paper cuts.

Little by little the body simply shuts down, as Denise so eloquently described in many of her blog posts.

As the body is affected, of course the mind can cave in as well. I think that's why the book Tuesdays with Morrie was so popular, because Morrie did not allow ALS to conquer his mind as well. Neither did my beloved.

As I've hopefully made clear in these pages, curbing and ultimately eliminating physical functions struck a greater blow on Denise and me because we were capital "A" active. Perhaps it was with a touch of anger that I decided to push Denise in her chair through eight marathons. ALS had taken enough. I would not allow it to spoil the joy we felt when running together.

In this closing chapter, Denise and I will take you deeper into our battle, homing in on the flesh-and-bone life as we continually adjusted to ever-decreasing functionality. ALS tried to beat us, to destroy us, to discourage us, but we just kept running-and I am still running, only with an empty chair in front of me now.

Here is one of Denise's early posts about how ALS literally knocked her off her feet and into my arms. "And So, It Goes" was written not long after Denise had that famous fall in her office.

"Days turned into weeks and weeks into months and I began to mark time with the changes in my mobility. Looking back, in January and February we were cross country skiing and ice skating, and I fell numerous times, as one would expect on the ice and snow, nothing really odd about that. Yet at my daughter's seventh birthday party, for the very first time she skated past me and said, 'Hey Mom, I can skate faster than you!' At the risk of sounding ruffled at the thought of being upstaged by a seven-year-old, I'd have to say something was wrong. You see, I had been rollerblading for nearly twenty years, and when I skated it was with speed not grace. I would always push myself to the limit, but on that day, something didn't feel right, and she passed me several times as I cautiously moved about the rink. I had just purchased a new pair of speed skates, and I was excited to use them for the first time, but I couldn't seem to find my groove. I wasn't sure if I just needed to get used to the skates or if something changed, but I took a hard fall and decided to step off for the day.

In March, I began to have increased pain in my right leg and lower back. I thought it was likely to be the bursitis I'd dealt with for the last twenty years aggravated by a tight IT band from the running workout I had been doing, so at the advice of a good friend I went to see an orthopedic back specialist. He examined me, prescribed an anti-inflammatory drug and physical therapy. In April and May I saw a PT and diligently did my exercises and stretches, but we couldn't seem to get rid of the pain, and I had developed a limp in my right leg, or as I later learned was called a gait disturbance.

I could still walk at a very brisk pace, but my right leg was slower than my left and it was noticeable.

On Memorial Day weekend the weather was beautiful and I decided to break out the rollerblades and try again. Maybe the wheels on my new skates were better on pavement than an indoor rink surface; I just needed traction! I skated cautiously, first in the garage, then the driveway and finally on the street in front of my house.

Back and forth, I focused on how I shifted my weight with my hips and heels. No quick turns or fancy stops, just an even stride and concentration on finding my groove. No luck, it must be these new skates; pull out the old K2's and get back up, try again, try harder; you can do this, the voice in my head continued to push me.

But the old skates did not revive my groove, and I wept on the floor of my garage knowing something that always brought me great joy was lost."

I hardly need to comment on this post. I can almost feel her warm tears running down her face and onto that garage floor as I held her there. As her husband, I knew that Denise had certain passions that brought her much joy.

Roller blading was certainly at the top of the list.

What do you most like to do? How would you feel if that passion was suddenly taken from you? The loss is enormous. It's a very personal assault.

ALS was on the march and began to steal so many potentially fun times that Denise and I had treasured, from cycling to jumping the waves on her beloved Jersey Shore. As a physical education teacher, I like to stay in shape and remain active. In the beginning I couldn't match Denise's fitness. She worked out a lot, and when we went for a walk, I needed to use my "survival shuffle" (which I have used in almost all of the forty-seven marathons I've completed) just to keep up with her.

The diminution of Denise's physical capabilities was swift. As the reality of our struggle began to settle in, two constant drags on the patient and caregiver threatened our happiness every day: 1) The truth that your loved one will indeed pass away from the malady, you just don't know when. That uncertainty/certainty presses on your heart and soul like a vise. It can squeeze the joy out of every day if you allow it to win. And, it is never far away; it can crush even the happiest times when it emerges. 2) The daily frustration of the disease changing you physically and altering your entire life and its routines. There is no glamor here, no photographers or reporters, just a lot of daily agony that worsens with time.

Denise wrote about the mushrooming physical challenges with her unfailing humor in a blog post entitled: "Where Did You Put the..."

"While I feel certain that I have adapted to my physical limitations, developing carefully sequenced routines, each new day presents its own set of challenges.

Now, before we go any further, I must confess that I have a self-diagnosed case of OCD; those of you who know me well can stop laughing... Translated that means: I have a fairly regimented approach to daily living so: 'Don't move anything from its proper place and I won't freak out' It's a pretty simple concept and one that, when embraced by those around me, leads to harmony in the home. Unfortunately, I can no longer fly through the house and accomplish tasks as quickly as I used to, so my well-intentioned family helps pick up the slack. Did I mention that each member of my family is uniquely gifted with their own sense of logic? This is important to note because later, when you are looking for something and it's not where it used to live for the last thirteen years, it would be helpful to understand how someone else arrived at the conclusion that the logical place to put that something was in the garage on a shelf that you can no longer get on a ladder to reach. Without this fundamental understanding and a sense of humor, the combination of ALS and OCD can be a recipe for wishing you had lost your mind too! On that note, I'd like to thank my sweet 8-year-old daughter for offering to carry my Blackberry downstairs for me this morning. Honey, next time, please don't take it to school with you...Mommy needs it."

Two qualities in any person make them particularly appealing: the ability to laugh at themselves and comfort with who they are. Both are plainly on display in this post. She found the light side in her brawl with ALS (somehow) and found even more amusement in how ALS hammered away at her OCD tendencies. Rather than shrivel up in self-pity, she poked fun at herself. Her blog posts are priceless and an outstanding guide for anyone who will face this giant.

Before we had the definitive ALS diagnosis, Denise was mystified both by her loss of agility and how deeply that would affect her relationships. In "Stealing Pieces" she detailed how confusing those days were for us both.

"Sometime earlier this year I received an e-mail about an exhibit called 'Stealing Pieces' on display at Daley Plaza in Chicago. I was curious, and so naturally I clicked on the link to see what it was about. There was a brief video that depicted what I can only vaguely recall as floating limbs. The idea was that little by little, ALS steals pieces of our loved ones. Remarkable! Someone had accurately described what I had been experiencing for nearly a year.

The previous June I could still run, although my right foot seemed to drop in an odd sort of way, but if I concentrated, I could give it that extra lift so I didn't lose my footing. I also had a difficult time climbing the Dunns River Falls in Jamaica that summer. Something I had done before with excitement now frightened me.

In July I decided that my sense of balance would make riding my bike scary, especially since I had changed out my pedals years ago to allow my shoes to lock into them. It required a certain amount of skillful control when stopping that I wasn't sure I could muster.

In August the Atlantic Ocean swept me off my feet with each gentle wave; I literally could not stand in the moving water. I grew up riding the waves on these beaches, and on this particular summer day they were tame and forgiving, and yet I could not hold myself up.

Still, I remember laughing it off... I'm not sure who I was trying to convince that it was nothing to worry about... me, my friends, my family? Anyway, we had an appointment scheduled in late August to see a neurologist; we'll figure this out when we get home and fix it... right?"

As we all came to discover, there was no "fixing it." ALS had invaded, set up shop, and was determined to steal so many precious pastimes that Denise treasured, from riding a bike to jumping waves. You get an idea of how active and vibrant she was—and why we were such a great match.

To go from a rollerblading/recreational jogging/fun-in-the-sun bundle of energy to having her bike taken away, then her roller blades, then her balance in the ocean. It all hurt. It was as if Denise's body was a hapless sports team on a long losing streak. Yet the beauty of her life is that she never viewed it all like that. She found delight in each day, and with each setback she doubled her courage and determination. Everyone around her saw this gutsy attitude that refused to surrender as she set her face like flint to live with this disease, not shrink before its terror. She was a continual inspiration to me and I will guard the memories of her bravery all the days of my life.

She was the most courageous woman I've ever known. She backed down from nothing-and that included her ALS diagnosis. The day after writing "Stealing Pieces," Denise was back at it, wanting to share more of her funny side as it related to private physical challenges, although this time she wrote about a few that had nothing to do with ALS. In "For Ladies Only" she wrote:

"FAIR WARNING: This one is for Ladies only!

Gentlemen, proceed with caution or you're likely to have the urge to put your fingers in your ears and run singing, la, la, la, la, la...' as I've seen so many of you do when the girl talk starts at the office; don't let this happen to you.

Many of my friends are in their late 40's, early 50's, so we've had our share of laughs surrounding our impending encounter with menopause, the anticipation and anxiety of the certain freak show we will embody, as our hormone levels rise and fall.

Did you know that there's actually a website that lists 34 potential symptoms of menopause? It's absolutely frightening! I won't trouble you with the entire list; I'm sure if you're reading this, you can Google it too.

I was familiar with many of the common ones, like: hot flashes, night sweats, irregular periods and mood swings, and I think we can all attest to the fact that by this time in our lives we've already experienced: memory lapses, anxiety, irritability and breast pain, but who's prepared for: burning tongue, electric shocks, incontinence, and... my all-time favorite on the list, 18. Change in Odor!

I'm gonna' dance on a twig and assume that's not a pleasant odor.

Seriously, I'd like to take a pass on menopause, I have enough on my plate...

Are you with me?"

Yes, that's right. Unfortunately, ALS does not exclude women of a certain age from the effects of menopause, but I didn't detect a change in Denise's odor! She always smelled lovely to me, and as far as her appearance went, she was just as beautiful as ever from the day we met and started our courtship. Call it what you like, but I call it "for better or worse," and in my mind there was no "worse" for the love of my life.

Her next post is one of my favorites. It condenses well the daily skirmish she fought and her customary humor in dealing with it. It also reveals a lot about Denise's priorities. She chose family over obsession regarding her personal appearance. This post also takes you into the world of adaptation that a person must master to perform even simple tasks as ALS encroaches.

Denise called this one, appropriately, "Frustrations."

"It's fairly easy to accumulate a growing list of frustrations as your previously obedient muscles no longer respond to visceral commands. Simple tasks you've always taken for granted like opening a plastic jar of peanut butter, removing the small square plastic thingy from the bag that contains your loaf of bread, and turning the knob on the fancy toaster you purchased at Williams and Sonoma, become an exercise in stamina and patience. You begin to question how badly you want that peanut butter and jelly sandwich, and consider that using your teeth to tear the wrapper off a protein bar, although barbaric, might be the easier way to go.

Additionally, you decide that it wouldn't be such a bad thing if the cleaning lady suddenly developed a mild case of OCD and straightened the artwork hanging on the walls after she dusted them. It's nice to know she's thorough, but does every piece need to be knocked off center just so I can obsess about it every Friday afternoon? I know, let it go... I'm pretty sure that someone else in this house will find it equally as irritating and set them level again anyway.

Then there's a whole list of frustrations related to dressing and undressing that make you want to live out the rest of your days in sweat pants and garments with Velcro closures. If you're home alone, the sports bra you can pull over your head is going to win hands down over that fancy lace bra with underwire... and since your legs don't seem to move with the same sense of urgency your bladder has assigned to the task of getting to the nearest bathroom, why button that top button on your jeans and create another obstacle to completing that performance when the time comes?

Grooming tasks in general present a challenge: tweezing, shaving, clipping your nails, even using a hair dryer, brush, or comb can be frustrating. A good haircut, a dab of gel and I'm letting Mother Nature take responsibility for the end result.

Forget about trying to put on mascara or eyeliner unless it's Halloween and it will be considered part of your costume, otherwise you're apt to frighten the children at the school bus stop with the mess you make of your face. A steady hand is required for that task and that's a thing of the past.

I realize it sounds like I've lowered the bar, and perhaps that's a little bit true, but some days you just have to pick your battles and save your energy for more important things like playing with your kids."

With or without makeup, Denise was gorgeous, but I understand women well enough to know that having to cut corners on personal appearance was not an easy compromise for her, even though she was never a vain person. If none of us cared at all about how we looked, then why do we look in the mirror every morning and make a few adjustments so that we look presentable? ALS forced shortcuts, as Denise described, and I was unable to fill in that gap.

That leads me to the topic of my role as a caregiver, one that perhaps many of you readers are taking on right now. As I consider my role in Denise's care, I must first issue a disclaimer: I was not the perfect caregiver for my wife. Looking back, I realize that I did so many things poorly. Those failures still keep me up at night, and honestly, they sometimes bring me to tears in the strangest times. The only truth that keeps me functioning in the day to day when I am haunted by the things I did wrong is the fact that Denise knew that I did my level best.

With that said, caregiving for a loved one is not for the faint of heart. There is no guidebook or Web site that tells you how to be a caregiver. Each situation is unique. The hardest part may be going from caring husband to caregiver, an unexpected jolt because those two roles are polar opposites. From diagnosis until the end of your loved one's life, everything in your life changes. And yes, I do know why a very high percentage of spouses, when faced with something of this magnitude, choose to simply leave the situation: I think in today's society that people have replaced "till death do us part" with "till times get tough." I had to stay true to Denise and the vow of marriage as God intended it to be. I played a huge part in messing up my first marriage and I was not going to let that happen again. I vowed to Denise to be all in, and that is exactly what I planned to do no matter what.

That nettlesome transition from husband to caregiver was quite a challenge.

I'm embarrassed to say that after a few years of caring for Denise, I forgot how to be a husband. I look at that as one of my biggest failings. Early on, I made the mistake of wanting to do everything for Denise, even doing things for her that she could have done on her own. I thought I was helping, but alas, I was doing the opposite. My Italian wife one day sat me down and told me exactly that. Her reasoning was that a month or two down the road, she may not be able to do what I was doing for her, tasks that she could have done on her own. Consequently, I was taking away her independence, which undoubtedly would eventually be taken away by the disease. She was so smart.

So, I listened and tried to do better. I enjoyed some success, but I still found myself doing things for her that she could have done. On a number of occasions, I got "the look" from her, not the googly-eyed "I love you so much" look, but the

"What the heck are you doing?" look. Many of my friends can attest to this as they witnessed firsthand those awkward situations.

The change that the diagnosis brought to my life continues to this day. I still always open the tops of water bottles for people without hesitation, even though they can absolutely do it for themselves. I avoid bread sold in packages with a plastic twist tie because that small wire wrapped in plastic frustrated Denise so much.

Another huge adjustment to being a caregiver was growing accustomed to a completely new rhythm of simply going from point A to point B. Let me explain: before ALS, when Denise and I wanted to go somewhere we just up and went, and Denise got ready remarkably quickly. Then, as the disease progressed, we needed to allow up to two or three hours just to prepare to go to a movie or even church.

Gone were the spontaneous road trips and romantic weekends

away, as we found it easier just to stay home, which wasn't all bad, as we had some great conversations about life.

In some ways we got closer as we navigated this disease, but I have to honestly say that the good never outweighed the bad. I'm not going to sugarcoat it.

As a caregiver you are on call 24-7. Of course, me being me, I felt I could handle it all myself. Read this next sentence carefully, future caregivers: I could not have been more wrong. This, I'm sure, led to some of the anger I found myself surrounded by at times. Don't get me wrong: I was never mad or angry at Denise.

The disease was what angered me so.

If you are a caregiver or about to become one, make sure you ask for help.

You will drive yourself crazy and struggle mightily as you battle the crippling effects of whatever malady you are confronting. You will also be surprised by how many people want to help but don't know how. We discovered this on multiple occasions, and you will be happy to discern it too. Don't fly solo. People actually desire to help you. Let them.

I could go on and on about caregiving and the ups and downs that go with it, but I think you get the idea. One thing you caregivers need to know is that you are a hero to the person for whom you are caring. Caregivers are the most selfless people around and that makes you heroic in my book.

On Election Day in November one year, I spoke to a group of caregivers in Madison, Wisconsin. I told them how important it was to also care for themselves, to find time to go for a walk, to play a round of golf or to meet up with friends for a cold one (or six). Regrettably I didn't do nearly enough of that early on because I felt I had to be with Denise all the time.

As I reflect, I realize that taking time for me wasn't just for my mental health, but that Denise also needed a break from me. Please make time for yourself. Not enough people do, which is why there are so many cases of burnout in caregivers.

Yes, your person needs you, but they need a healthy you (in mind, body, and spirit) more than anything.

Providentially for me, Denise was an ideal receiver of care who did not allow herself to wallow in a pool of defeatism. Not even the scariest tests could diminish my wife's upbeat attitude. You may remember an earlier post referring to spinal taps. About a week after recounting her experience in the MRI tube, she gave a firsthand look at what spinal taps are all about in "Spinal Taps Are Not Fun."

"I realize I've been jumping around and my post 'Still Searching for Answers,' left off in late August, early September 2010, so let me take the time to catch you up.

We saw the neurologist at the end of August, after the initial tests came back from the orthopedic. He performed a neurological exam that vaguely resembles a sobriety test, only you're not worried because: he's not a cop, he didn't pull you over, and you haven't had any adult beverages before the appointment. He didn't say much during the exam, he uttered physical commands; I complied. He asked some questions, I answered and he concluded that it was all very perplexing. He needed more information so he ordered additional blood tests, another MRI, a test called Evoked Potentials, and finally a SPINAL TAP.

What I learned over the nine months of poking and prodding was that all of these tests were performed in succession to rule out one horrifying disease after another.

So, while we were happy when these tests came back negative, it was like blissful ignorance, as they upped the ante with even more horrifying options, as you played Spin the Wheel of Fate to see which debilitating disease we will land on.

The MRI was no big deal, been there, done that, nap time in the noisy cocoon. I passed both types of evoked potentials with flying colors, a few electric shocks but relatively tame. Then came the dreaded spinal tap; this one scared me and my instincts did not fail me.

It suffices to say that the spinal tap was unsuccessful even after multiple attempts.

While I lay face down on a cold metal table that could be tilted to the point of standing me upright, a team of four used an x-ray machine, a needle, and gravity to coax spinal fluid to leave my body. That was followed up with spinal fluid leaking from the two pin holes they created in my lower back within 48 hours of returning home. This leaking causes the pressure in your brain to drop, leaving you with the mother of all headaches and the inability to hold down so much as a drop of water.

The spinal tap was on Friday, and by Tuesday we were heading back to the hospital, to the emergency room this time, to get a blood patch, a procedure that uses blood they take from your arm to seal the two leaking lumbar punctures in your lower back that would not produce the spinal fluid in the first place. This procedure also required a room full of medical professionals. Oh, and since you're already here, the doctor would like us to take some more blood for additional tests.

We later learned that those additional blood tests indicated that I had been exposed to a Lyme antibody; apparently it was also present in a previous series of tests but it seemed unusual, so the test was done a second time. Armed with another positive test result for Lyme antibodies, the neurologist referred us to an infectious disease specialist, and so the next leg of the journey begins..."

And so it went, from doctor to doctor, from test to test, from mystery to mystery. Again, I think the mental aspect of our walk through the Valley of Death was at least as difficult as the physical trials. Onto the Lyme disease doctor we went, a visit that Denise chronicled in "Germbusters."

"We were referred to Germbusters, a catchy name for the practice, and the doctor was known to be a Lyme's Disease specialist, born, raised and educated on the East Coast, where the disease was first discovered.

He was a pleasant fellow, happy to meet another transplant, and we bonded as we shared commonalities reaching as far back as our grandparents coming from nearby towns in Italy. He took my history, including where I was born, lived, and traveled over my 40-plus years. While the tests were not 100% conclusive, he was fairly certain that my East Coast upbringing and ongoing trips back to the homeland qualified me for the likelihood that one of those nasty little ticks had at some point gotten to me.

Fortunately, Lyme's Disease was treatable if caught early, but there was no telling how long ago the alleged interlude might have occurred, and left untreated the bacteria had the potential to cause all kinds of neurological problems.

He was confident in his ability to kill the little spirochetes and described his aggressive treatment plan that included inserting a central line through a vein in your arm straight into your heart, to pump the antibiotic into your bloodstream daily for six weeks. There was no time to waste, and while he did not promise that I would return to normal after the treatment, he could prevent further damage by annihilating them.

So, okay…I have Lyme's Disease, that's not too bad, and back to the hospital we go to have a central line installed. Interesting procedure, not for the squeamish, but it was over quickly, and it wasn't too painful. Next, were off to the clinic to learn how to administer the drug myself once a day. The nurse in the infusion clinic patiently showed me the six steps to be followed precisely to ensure I would not develop an infection. I would return to see her weekly and she would give me the week's allotment of medication, check the port and take blood for testing.

This wasn't too bad. I had to repeat the process the same time each day, so I did it at lunch time. This did occasionally throw people who walked into my office during the 30-minute event, if they weren't aware of my new ritual. But they got used to it as quickly as they did when, for a span of time, I sat on a large lime green balance ball instead of my office chair. Just for fun I'd bounce up and down while working at my desk and catch the confused look on the face of a passerby that did a double take to see what in the world, I was up to… sometimes you have to make your own fun at work!

When we had completed four weeks of treatment, I saw the doctor to evaluate the progress. 'How are you feeling?' he asked. 'Good, maybe a little tired but nothing dramatic while taking the drug so far,' I replied. He looked down, with a sort of melancholy look on his face that puzzled me. The insurance company only pays for four of his aggressive six-week plan, so given the considerable out-of-pocket expense, I asked if he thought I would benefit from the additional two weeks of treatment.

Apparently, not feeling worse indicated that nothing was happening, and if the drug was actually killing those little spirochetes, I would have been feeling awful as they fought back. He concluded that he did not think I would benefit from the additional medication, and there was nothing more he could do for me. He actually looked defeated as he referred me back to the neurologist.

So, back to the hospital to remove the central line...

I guess it wasn't Lyme's Disease after all..."

Back down in the valley, trying to find reasons and solutions. Yet Denise refused to dwell in the doldrums. She even found purpose in our futile two months under the assumption of her carrying Lyme's disease in her body, as she mentions below. But we were about to hear a diagnosis far more serious than Lyme's. We were about to hear three letters that no one should hear. Denise explained this in her next blog post called "Back to the Drawing Board."

"Okay, so it's not Lyme's Disease, but I learned a new skill: I could inject antibiotics into a central line... and who knows when that may come in handy?

We met with the neurologist again and he explained that he had some ideas about what was going on, but he would need to perform one more test to confirm his suspicions. He could perform the test himself, in his office.

So, on December 9, 2010, we returned to his office for an EMG, short for Electromyogram. After careful consideration, I can report without hesitation that an EMG is even more painful than a spinal tap, save the week-long aftermath. This uncomfortable procedure involves placing electrodes in several strategic locations on your body: arms, legs, feet, and spine, while the doctor performs tests to evaluate the health of your nerves and muscles.

He begins with something called a Nerve Conduction Study, in which he measures nerve function by stimulating them with small electric shocks, not too bad, similar to the Evoked Potentials testing, only more extensive, but it doesn't end there…

In part two, he inserts a needle equipped with a microscopic electrode into your muscles, and as if that's not painful enough, he moves it around while you flex the muscle being tested. Did I say 'OUCH'? When he stuck the needle in my back, my body jumped so high it left the table! For Pete's sake…what did I do to deserve this kind of torture? Okay, I did accidentally kill my brother's gerbil when I was eleven, but he bit me, and it was not intentional; it was self-defense!

When it was over and the doctor left the room, I could see by the look on my husband's face that it was just as painful to watch as it was to actually be the pin cushion. I dressed and we waited for the doctor to return with his diagnosis.

It was surreal, like a scene from one of those medical TV shows you've watched. I could see his lips moving but the words hung in the air as if I could just refuse to accept them into my reality. ALS meant nothing to me…Lou Gehrig's disease? He was a baseball player, he died, but that was a long time ago… Two to five years…

Seriously? I looked over at my husband and saw his eyes filled with tears but I held out. Surely this can't be right."

Once the diagnosis sunk in, it explained a lot. Then came the hard and harder part. With this chapter covering the physical challenges of ALS, one simple action that you may not think about revolves around the most basic movements all of us do simply to stay alive: eat. You know, like picking up a fork and spoon and stuffing our faces?

Well, for an ALS patient, that can get very complicated and difficult. It worsens when you are around lots of other people and not wanting to make a scene. And, it can get even more frustrating when you are sitting around a table with scrumptious food, like at holiday time, that delicious period from late November to New Year's Day.

But rather than crack up, Denise poked fun at herself again as she detailed her struggles with cutting food and getting it into her mouth and stomach. Enjoy

"My Table Manners Are Appalling!" and see again what a remarkable woman she was. (In contrast, I would have probably written a post about throwing every item off the table onto the wall in anger!)

"I'd like to apologize to those of you who have had to sit through a meal with me recently. While I am still the proud owner of a copy of Tiffany's Table Manners for Teenagers, had you the experience of watching me try to employ the use of common utensils, such as a fork, spoon, or heaven forbid, a knife, you would think I was raised by a pack of wolves.

I realize it doesn't help dispel the allegation, when I try to pry the cap off the bottled water with my teeth, but the rubber band trick I was using no longer works for me. It seems that between the loss of fine motor skills and muscle tone, even a spoon is not safe in my hands, and most foods simply do not defy gravity long enough to stay on the utensil until reaches my mouth. Luckily some gets in, but the rest either falls on my plate, the newly laundered tablecloth, the napkin in my lap, or if Blue is really lucky it goes straight to the floor.

This ongoing struggle has played out in several ways: it takes me a really long time to eat; I am usually tired and still hungry by the time I give up. Chris will sometimes cut my food for me, which is thoughtful at home, but could become embarrassing if we start to do it in public. Blue eagerly awaits his just rewards during dinner, and on a happy note I weigh less than what's printed on my driver's license, and how many of us can honestly say that?

I bring this up because... well, now that it's November and the holiday season will soon be upon us, some of you may want to take this into consideration before adding me to your guest list for a holiday gathering. Or, if you are willing to take the chance, be prepared to find me a dimly lit place, away from your nice china and throw me some finger foods.

Don't worry if it's a more formal setting, I can still remember to discreetly check my hands under the table so I don't mistakenly use the wrong bread plate or water glass...

I've lost control of motor functions, not my good sense."

I smile as I read that post, remembering Denise's class and grace. ALS did not rob her of either of those. Boy, did I marry up!

As Denise's symptoms worsened, she not only struggled to feed herself, she had to cut back on her writing, which really bothered her. She even apologized to those who followed her blog, although no apology was necessary. Denise slowed down her writing pace not just due to ALS, but to other physical problems that were, of course, exacerbated by ALS. Yet she spent minimal time in self-pity, thinking instead of those she supposedly let down when she wasn't able to bang out a post every day on the keyboard.

Here is "I'm No Slacker."

"It's been a rough week or so, and I have to admit I just haven't had the energy to write... But I would hate for any of you to think I was just slacking off, so I'm going to try to fill you in between naps.

On top of my everyday physical challenges with ALS, I've been in the throes of my semi-annual allergy attack which involves: head congestion, sinus pressure, a nose that runs like a leaky faucet, a choking cough driven largely by a post-nasal drip, and a case of what my doctor refers to as Eustachian Tube Dysfunction (ETD). Yet another incurable disorder I managed to score in the gene pool, that will often cause me to stick my fingers in my ears at what might seem to be an inappropriate moment.

In short, my head feels like a lead balloon and every orifice within it is clogged in some fashion. My former co-workers can attest to witnessing this event in the Spring and Fall of every year; it is most notably recognized by the choking cough that is about as pleasant to listen to as nails on a chalkboard. I assure you; it is as annoying for the choke-ee as it is for those unfortunate enough to be in earshot.

Now, there are some OTC and Rx options that can help manage the symptoms until a lasting frost kills off the allergens, but these remedies often zap me into another stratosphere.

Pre-ALS, taking these medications often made me loopy, but I remained somewhat functional, meaning I could take them after I arrived at work, as to avoid operating heavy machinery while drug induced, and get through the day fairly well. I would likely be more amusing than usual under these conditions, and the worst thing I can remember happening was when I accidentally headed into the men's room instead of the ladies' room. No worries, I caught myself in time...

Post-ALS, the combination of my regular medications and those that help manage my allergies simply knock me out. I find myself falling asleep while sitting at my PC, waking only to realize two hours have essentially evaporated.

I'm usually up early, but since there's no school this week, I took the liberty of sleeping in the past few days to try to get some extra rest. I wake surrounded by small creatures trapping me beneath the covers: Crabby the kitty sleeps off my left shoulder; Nik, a larger kitty is planted directly on my chest, and to my right competing for space lay Maddie, my adorable eight-year-old, with Blue, our jealous Border Collie mix, sprawled across her tiny body to rest his head on my right shoulder.

Nik and Blue take turns licking my face, and Nik sneaks an occasional nip on my nose, until I pull one of my otherwise pinned arms out from under the covers and give in to petting them. And so another day begins...by the time I get up, shower, dress and take my meds, I'm about two hours away from a nap...

So much as cold temperatures are not my preference, I would be pleased with a nice frost to put an end to current unproductive schedule."

That post gives a hint at Denise's frustration as ALS changed her from a fitness fanatic to a napper, quite a transformation and very hard to swallow for a perpetually productive person like her. Along with her difficulties in fighting allergies were challenges with other basic functions. As you would suppose, ALS doesn't just impact the easy-to-see parts of our body. It reaches into all muscles, including those that keep us regular and enable us to get rid of waste in a normal adult way. But life was becoming anything but normal for Denise, and as she hilariously recounts in the next post, she commenced a battle with her bladder.

Here again is a shining example of an open and honest person who is secure enough with herself to share with the world her bladder issues. Psychologists tells us that people love people who are honest, even if that honesty can make others uncomfortable. No wonder Denise was so well loved!

Read now "Time to Call the Plumber!"

"Okay, there's no getting through this without grace, humility, and lots of humor...

So, it was time to put on my big girl panties and call the plumber.

Going back about fourteen months, I began to notice a sense of urgency. At the time we were still playing 'What's My Disease?' and for the moment I was being treated for Lyme's Disease, with a daily regimen of self-administered antibiotics via a central pic line in my arm. I was told the medication was strong and it could have side effects, so just in case, I mentioned my symptoms to the nurse on my weekly visit; we ran some tests but nothing turned up.

Months passed and we had a name for my disease, but I was told it spared the plumbing, so I occasionally requested another test, but to no avail. This pattern continued for a few more months until I decided to ask my gynecologist on my annual visit. She asked a few questions, drew me a rough sketch of the female parts while providing something of an anatomy lesson, using phrases like 'This is where the pee is, and this is where the poop is.'

Seriously, I can't manufacture fodder this entertaining; perhaps I appeared to have arrived via the short bus, in any case it was amusing. She ordered more tests and referred me to someone better equipped to help me with my problem: the plumber.

Apparently, plumbers of human pipes are as busy as the regular ones, so I was offered the first available appointment some six weeks later, and my problem continued to worsen. My legs were progressively becoming harder to move and my bladder harder to control; this was heading in a bad direction.

Finally, the day came and I was filled with hope that relief from this socially unacceptable behavior was within reach. The doctor looked a bit like Christina Yang on "Grey's Anatomy" and projected a much kinder disposition; the combination was both comforting and reassuring in odd way as I lay exposed for examination. She poked around in much the same fashion as her predecessor, with a new twist...

'A Kegel? Sure, I know what that is... Oh, you want me to do some now? Of course, I can do that. Yes... I know it's not a leg exercise, let me try again. Sheesh! I'm glad we cleared that up...'

She described a few different ways bladder issues can present in patients, some of the likely causes and respective treatments, none for which I felt any particular kinship. And most certainly not the one where she surgically creates some kind of flap to support a worn-out muscle; I'll do Kegels from sunup to sundown to avoid attending that surgical event!

So, she explained, we will start with some medication and see how that works, and if that doesn't help, there are some additional tests we can set up. One is a flow test and the other is a Urodynamic study, but let's wait on the Big Fancy test; we won't do that if the medication works.

The nurse came in to follow up with the RX, provide paperwork that describes the two tests that would be possible, next steps, along with my homework assignment: a Void Diary. That was a clever name for a journal to record every ounce of intake and output, including any spillage along the way...

So now I had to document the whole embarrassing ordeal and return with my shameful diary, but it didn't end there!

Stay tuned for the next episode when we explore The Big Fancy Test!"

ALS will rob you of your dignity if you let it, but that was another commodity that Denise never let it steal. That's another reason why I loved her so much. She clung to so many of the essentials that made her who she is. ALS changed her completely on the outside, but she never allowed it to touch her inner person. In fact, if it were possible, her inner person became even more beautiful.

"The Big Fancy Test" that Denise referred to above was detailed in her next post a few weeks later. I noticed that she wrote this one on January 1%. To bring herself some joy as 2012 began, Denise used her gifts and intellect to make the rest of us laugh. In her post "Always Looking Sexy," Denise posits that ALS does not stand for those three words, but ALS or no ALS, my wife always appealed to me.

Her beauty truly flowed from the inside and shone throughout our years together, as you can tell from these winsome entries.

"When we got home from the last plumbing appointment, I read through the paperwork describing the two tests that would be potential next steps and decided the prescription was going to have to work!

I began taking the medication and tried to convince myself it was working, but three weeks later I was still unsure that anything had changed. I took some time to research the medication online and read that you could take as much as 10mg daily, and I was only at 5mg. So, I decided to call and ask if we could increase the dosage, hoping that would work. I was given the green light and informed that sometimes the medication took time to work and to give it a few weeks.

Wanting desperately to avoid the tests, I increased the dosage and willed myself to believe it was making a difference... but in the end, in the battle of mind over matter, my will could not prevail, and embarrassing events began to occur more often than I'd like to admit.

It had gotten to the point that I had to seriously limit my fluid intake, especially if I dared to push my luck and leave the house, but it really wasn't the best solution, as the lack of fluids in general made me feel worse.

While at the clinic for a study visit, a sample was requested, and since I was unable to comply, I had to admit to my less-than-brilliant strategy of fluid limitation. I was warned of the harmful effects of dehydration and encouraged to utilize protective products to deal with the situation. After all, these high-tech garments were invented for the astronauts, there's no reason why I should be embarrassed about using them!

Oh sure... Use the high-tech argument with the geek! Just because I like computers and software doesn't mean I'd be eager to wear Depends! However, I had to humbly admit I needed to try some kind of a protective garment, at the very least when out of the house for extended periods of time.

Okay, so the way I figured it, the most discreet way to handle this would be shopping for them on the Internet, and Amazon.com seemed to carry everything I've needed so far, and the search commenced.

I wasn't prepared for the expansive selection, and the attempts at persuasive marketing to lure potential buyers. Although I needed them, it was apparent to me that I was not their target customer when I felt no excitement after reading Now in new soft peach!'

The product features were interesting:

'Size: small/medium fits 115-190 lbs'—This was of concern to me; how is it possible that one garment could properly fit individuals that range 75 lbs. in body weight?

Two ways to change: step-in & pull-up OR easy change with 4

secure Velcro closures, sounded too much like the description on diapers for toddlers.

'Maximum absorbency, captures and locks in odor,' okay, sounds useful...

'Quiet and comfortable,' you mean to tell me these make noise when you wear them? That ought to be hilarious!

'Made in the USA from domestic and imported materials'... Seriously?

And 'Unisex?' It's been a while since I had to purchase diapers for my daughter, but I do remember them being gender specific. Why would that change for adults?

At any rate... I had to make a choice, and none of the options were going to come close to matching my favorite French lace bras, so I had to find some way to have fun when it came time for a dry run with my new undergarments. And well... wearing my matching panties over the soft peach granny pants doesn't mean I've lost my mind, it's just an example of my resilient sense of humor!

Sorry, Honey... ALS does not stand for Always Looking Sexy!"

It says something about our skewed human nature that we would be so interested in the most personal matters of a person battling a powerful disease.

Yet, Denise sensed two facts about her readers: that they did indeed want to hear more about her adventures with adult undergarments and they were interested in the so-called "Big Fancy Test." She satisfied the curiosity of us all with her next entry: "The Dry Run."

"While I realize many of you may be thinking it's time to move on to another topic and put the potty issues behind us... believe me when I tell you, I share your sentiments and would have liked to report that the dilemma was resolved, but that has not been the case. So, hang in there, and try to summon the courage to continue reading. You may find yourself wanting to look away, but feeling compelled to peek the way you do when passing a car wreck...

The private garments arrived via the Internet, and so the day came when I ventured out, fully outfitted for the Dry Run! I'd like to point out that this was an attempt to gauge comfort and feasibility, with the expectation to be somewhat uneventful and to quite literally experience a dry run, pun intended!

I had no such luck, and learned quickly that I could not depend on Depends to fit my bottom snugly enough to hold the inevitable deluge...proving my theory that they could not possibly work for everyone between 115-190 lbs. Not having planned for the possibility of a wet run, at the age of 49, I had my first ever Commando experience. You can stop laughing now!

Desperate for a solution, I finally called to schedule 'The Big Fancy Test' I had been avoiding. The directions for test preparation included arriving with a full bladder.

Really? You must be joking! If I had the ability to arrive with a full bladder and not lose control, I would not need the test! I opted for sipping some water on the ride there, in hopes that some would make it to my bladder before the test began; this appeared to suffice.

The technician who performed the test was very pleasant and explained the procedure in detail before she began inserting tiny long tubes with electronic sensors in very private places. Once again humbled by the embarrassment of my business exposed, and with the added pleasure of being wired to measure fluid levels and contractions, I decided this was the equivalent of having Chris in the delivery room, had we shared the experience of the birth of a child. This was a new level of intimacy that would certainly enhance our marriage...good grief!

Although I still maintain the opinion that a non-invasive catheter is an oxymoron, when it was all over and done with, I'd have to admit it was not that bad. I'd been through worse, and I had minimal discomfort following the procedure.

Two weeks later we met with the doctor, our own Christina Yang, and learned that my overactive bladder was contracting intensely when it was filled far below capacity, but it was otherwise functioning normally. Since the medication I was taking was not helping, there were two others I could try before resorting to more radical approaches to resolving the problem.

She went on to describe a procedure where they use a pacemaker to regulate the nerve impulses that cause the contractions, and although that sounded interesting, I was still hoping one of the two medications we had yet to try would do the trick.

In the meantime, the nurse suggested we try the XL size kids Pull Ups, as I would likely fit into the size range and prevent leakage in the event of another incident.

Another two weeks have passed since I started the new medication and I am happy to report that it appears to be working. Unfortunately, there were some side effects I should have paid more attention to that resulted in an unscheduled visit to the ER last week, but with extra fluids and an extra-large bowl of Raisin Bran every day, I hope to avoid a sequel to that unpleasant trauma...

While the Pull Ups with the cute butterflies, hearts, and peace signs are much easier to laugh about, I'm ready to give them up now... So, let's hope this is the last you'll hear of my dysfunctional plumbing; I think we're ready for some new material..."

More than a month after that post, Denise did shift gears, both literally and metaphorically. I had batted around the idea of including her in my training runs for marathons and also signing her up to run with me in races as I pushed her chair. I had a feeling that Denise would revel in being outdoors as she was reminded of the joy she felt while rollerblading. For that reason, I chose her favored path to do my own training runs. She wrote a beautiful tribute to our first run together entitled, "Training Rides." It was the first of many, and those times together are some of my most precious memories.

"This week I was finally able to get out into the sunshine and ride along with Chris on his training runs, and I could see right away why our proxy riders, Maddie and Amber, were enjoying the experience. Wow, fresh air, sunshine, and someone to push while I just sit back and savor the thrill of the ride, this is delightful!

First, I thought... I'd very selfishly claim the blessing of the mildest winter weather I can recall in my experience in Chicagoland, as God's favor on our quest...and why not? After all, on a beautiful June day in 2010, our beach wedding got rained out, as a severe thunderstorm passed through the area at the exact time it was to commence. Four months later, a very large deer ran into our brand new CRV, nearly totaling it. Did I mention, this happened while we were on our way to church? And... two months later, we got the news that I had ALS!

Through it all my faith and my sense of humor, have stayed remarkably intact, so I say sunny 40-degree weather in Chicagoland in February is gift intended just for us, and I dare you to argue the point, no matter how crazy or delusional it sounds to you. Stake your own claims...I won't stand in your way.

I was elated that Chris chose to run my old rollerblade route, a three-mile loop I would repeatedly race around to the point of exhaustion, at any opportunity during the warmer months. Still... my personal best at seven laps or 21 miles, would be shy of Chris' challenge to push me 26.2 in May. I've been joking about needing a blindfold for the marathon knowing how fast Chris can run, but I really wouldn't want to miss one moment of the experience.

Chris shares the excitement of his riders, so it seems that he likes to have a chatty passenger, but for me, the relationship with the course was much too intimate to divert my focus with conversation.

You see... it had been two summers since I'd felt the vibrations from the wheels against the pavement, and as they were emanating from the footboard where my feet were tethered, they were pulling me back into the memory. I closed my eyes, focused on the movement of the jogger, and slipped back into my skates to savor the run.

I didn't have to open my eyes to know that we were winding down Saddleridge, or headed downhill on Bridle. I could still feel the burn in my quads as we pushed up Old Forge and Appaloosa, and I giggled when he took the steep winding path by the park at full speed.

This was more than a training run for me; it was a chance to feel a little bit of the joy I used to feel under my feet; it was a wonderful gift, and I can't wait to get back out there.

Thank you, Chris..."

You are more than welcome, Honey! It was my pleasure.

Those training runs would lead to much greater feats of endurance and perseverance, some of which attracted a lot of attention. In fact, one aspect of this arduous passage of life that I'm most proud of was our ability to make many people aware of the fight for a cure, as newspapers, television stations, magazines, and Web sites heard about our story. I guess the drama of a guy pushing his wife for 26.2 miles in a chair was kind of unusual; I'm sure that Denise's charisma was unusual.

To rally people around our cause we needed to get in racing shape. I had made promises to Denise about running and competing, and I was going to keep those promises, ALS be damned. One of those vows was to run a marathon with her, one way or another, a goal we had made before her diagnosis. For Denise especially, and me to some extent, her prognosis was not going to stop us.

Once it became clear that Denise would not be able to run, I figured if we couldn't run the "normal" way the next best thing would be to push her, to at least give her a feel of experiencing a marathon from start to finish. By the grace of God, the Les Turner Foundation purchased a jogger for us, a sporty chair on wheels, and training commenced. I had never pushed anything while running, so I first pushed the empty jogger to get used to it. Pushing is totally different than running!

As runners we take our arms for granted and don't realize how they assist us while running. That's why pushing the jogger was such an adjustment for me. After a few dry runs, I added Maddie to the jogger to have an actual human being inside and to add a little weight. She absolutely loved it and smiled the whole time she was inside. Then finally, I put Amber in. She was a great sport about it, and as luck would have it, she was about the same size as Denise. All of these preparatory steps were also done to ensure that my most precious cargo-Denise--would be safe before I put her in the chair.

I remember the first time Denise and I went for a training run. We planned on going for a short three-miler on her rollerblade course she loved but she was so ecstatic about being out and moving that we ended up doing a nine-miler, three times around the course she loved so much. She just wanted to keep going and I wasn't going to stop.

The training runs that followed were some of the best times of our short life together. My only complaint was that Denise pushed me well beyond my capability as a runner! She used to rollerblade the same trail and she was so fast. As we progressed around her course I kept checking if she was okay, and all she did was to motion for me to go faster. She loved going fast.

Some of those hills were downright scary as we shot down them. Denise truly had a need for speed. It was so fun. Many times, I needed the dreaded ice bath after a training run with her. It was so worth it for my body to be beat up a bit. Her smile told it all. We've trained in extreme heat, snow, and rain. Her favorite was training in the heat. She was a Jersey girl and she loved the sun. She even had a sticker on her wheelchair that said, "Of course I'm tanned, I'm from Jersey." She had the time of her life when our training runs were in the sun.

As we trained, we grew closer and closer. It seemed the miles we put in together did good for both of us. For Denise, she felt alive, sensing the wheels under her as the miles passed by. For me, it gave me purpose and the opportunity to share one of my passions with my wife. The progression of the disease presented us with some challenges but it never slowed us down. The time we spent training was sacred. We were two people lost in each other as we ran together.

I believe our training runs gave us a solid foundation to do battle with this disease. There was nothing that was going to stop us from our goal of running a marathon together. I need to give a shout-out to the Les Turner Foundation, a nonprofit organization serving ALS patients in the Chicago area. A wonderful woman named Kim McIver helped Denise and I decide on our first marathontogether.

Of course, it would be New Jersey, Denise's home state. Better yet, it would be along the shore where she had spent so much time growing up.

Typical of the type of selfless love we were shown throughout Denise's final years, the foundation even purchased our first racing chair for the event. Each marathon was difficult for me as I was deprived of my normal arm movements used to propel all of us as we run, but Denise's joy made it worth any sacrifice that I made. I think she really felt like she was alive again when she was being pushed and the crowds yelled for us. All you have to do is take a look at the photos of me pushing Denise during these races. Her smile is as broad as the horizon in Big Sky country.

The Daily Herald, Chicago's largest suburban paper, wrote a great article on that first race together, featuring some of the humor that Denise specialized in. The reporter, Jessica Cilella, pointed out that Denise had to be awakened from a deep nap at mile marker 25. I woke her up because we had a plan to include Leah and Maddie in the last 2/10 of a mile. That was unforgettable as well.

As Cilella reported, "Her face broke into a smile. Dozens of friends and family members cheered as the couple crossed the finish line... fulfilling a dream to one day run a marathon together despite DiMarzo's eighteen-month fight with amyotrophic lateral sclerosis. 'It was a day filled with hope and love; I will never forget it!' DiMarzo wrote in an e-mail after the race."

Our first New Jersey Marathon. Meredith
and Kyle were the best throughout.

I chimed in, "It was awesome. It was not only the most difficult marathon of my life, but it also was just the best because Denise could share it with me." Ms.

McIver, who had done so much to make our race possible also gave her insight,

"Chris wanted to make a statement with this race. He wants people (touched by ALS) to know that you can still achieve your goals together."

I'm sure that we did make a statement, and the $28,000 we raised as a result proved that. Yet again, however, I must give credit to friends who helped pull us through this stiff test of our will. As I told the Daily Herald, "It was hard on me and my friends Meredith (Kline) and Kyle (Mitchell). They pulled me along. They weren't about time, they were about staying with us and sharing the experience." Kyle was a coworker who ran with his girlfriend, Meredith, and made our group an overachieving quartet that day. That's true friendship!

There's nothing better in a race than seeing that finish line, and Ms. McIver hit the nail on the head when she told the reporter, "Everybody was relieved that they finished and they accomplished their goal. They definitely woke the crowd upwhen they were going through the finish line." That relief included me, and no, I will never forget those cheers of solidarity. They humbled me greatly and do to this day.

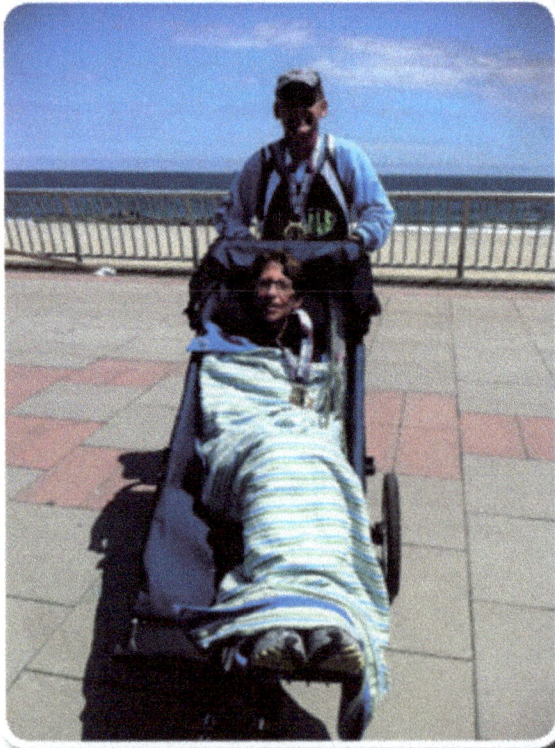

Denise and my finish picture from our 1st marathon ever. Such a beautiful setting.

As I pointed out to the paper, "We're just trying to make our best out of a bad situation, and I guess people find that inspirational." My guess proved correct as we continued to attract media attention everywhere we raced. The Les Turner Foundation even named us its "Patient/Family of the Year" in 2012, which led to a photo shoot for the July 2012 Runner's World magazine.

Who knows how many people were inspired by seeing me push Denise for four or five hours at a time in races around the country? All I know is what I told Ms. Cilella, "It was better than we ever expected it to be."

We did a total of eight marathons together, including Boston in 2014 and 2016. Because of Denise's faith, we were able to do something together that could be called nothing other than a miracle, given our situation. I often wonder how Denise could stay so positive and be in the fight of her life for five-plus years. I don't think I could have done it. She showed us all perseverance, strength, determination, grace, dignity, love, and most importantly that the life we are given is a gift we should never take for granted.

As I wrote for the Muscular Dystrophy Association's "Strongly" Web site in reflecting on our races together, "God truly smiled down on me that day in the fall of 2009 when I met her. Although I miss her terribly, I always try to remember her spirit, her infectious smile and her sense of humor. All I have are memories and her pictures in a frame. I know God has her in his arms. I will always have her in my heart."

For a peek into Denise's mind as I pushed her 26.2 miles, I share a blog post she did that documented her feelings after we ran our second New Jersey Marathon together. It had been more than a year since Denise had released a post.

This is another entry that could have served as a title for this book: "Smiling through the Pain."

"It was a brisk, sun-filled morning on the Jersey shore. We were fortunate to have intimate knowledge of the back roads in the local towns, and made it to the start in record time. We advanced through the parking lot to the entrance of Monmouth Park, as if we had backstage passes to a rock concert. Shortly after we arrived, we spotted Eric, with his distinct mohawk hair cut, new to the team this year, he added his own flash of excitement. This was going to be fun!

Huddled in the van to stay warm, waiting for the rest of our teammates to get through the long line of vehicles pouring into the lot, you could feel the nervous energy. Chris called out to Nancy and Dani, two of our half marathoners, racing to the starting line as it was beginning. We exchanged quick hugs, and they were off!

Soon after, Laura, Meredith, and Kyle came trotting over, and it was time to open the door, and roll down the ramp. The controls had recently been changed on my power wheelchair, and admittedly, I was still trying to get the hang of it. Chris eased me down carefully, and in a snap, they transferred me from the chair into the jogger. Harnessed in, we headed for the last corral at the start. We were not looking to set any records that day; it was about the journey, not the finish time.

This was the third year we were returning to the New Jersey Marathon. Although Chris ran it in 2011, he ran it alone, while my sister Angie, and cousin MJ, pushed me in a wheelchair to catch a glimpse of him at as many check points as possible. It was a sight to behold, two middle aged women pushing a third, as fast as possible, uphill then downhill, laughing hysterically! I cannot imagine what the people we passed were thinking, but we had a blast cheering Chris on at every opportunity.

Having been diagnosed five months earlier Amyotrophic Lateral Sclerosis (ALS), I could still walk short distances, but my running days were over.

In 2012, Chris ran while pushing me in the jogger, Meredith and Kyle joined us for the full marathon, while a group of nine other friends and family members ran the half. Kyle, also taught Physical Education, like my husband Chris, and Meredith, a former third grade student of his, was all grown up and teaching too. I love to tease him about it, because it makes Chris feel old. They had plenty to talk about during the race, and well... I was as snug as a bug in a rug, and managed to fall asleep for a bit after mile ten. Something Chris will never let me forget!

This year, 2013, was very different, Super Storm Sandy had ravaged the coastline at the end of 2012, and my disease had progressed leaving its crippling effect on my body. Neither of us would ever be the same physically, but our spirits were not broken!

We started out slowly, at the back of the crowd of runners lining the start. A place, I'm certain, my veteran, marathon husband, has never before seen, and I promised myself, to stay awake the entire 26.2 miles. It was the first chance I had to see the shore since the storm, and I didn't want to miss a mile. As we traversed the course, vivid images of my childhood ran through my mind, followed by my first car, first apartment, and many memories of my adult life. I found myself once again, questioning why I had ever left.

I enjoyed listening to the banter flying back and forth between the runners.

Meredith and Kyle were weeks away from their wedding, Laura was running her first full marathon, and Eric had a witty sense of humor. Given that they were all good friends, there was plenty of material with which to do a stand-up routine as they razzed each other, and kept me entertained through the whole event.

Having been awake for every mile this year, I learned that marathon runners go through phases as the miles tick away. They start out pumped up, filled with adrenaline, calling out the mile markers as they approach. "That's three!", "That's six!", "That's ten…", "Looking good!", they cheered, while passing Shot Blocks and Goo for energy, and stopping briefly for port-a-pottys, Gatorade, water, or to thank a random citizen with a shout-out as we passed.

Another big difference this year was that Chris allowed the team to participate in the hardest part of the race, pushing me! I know that was a tough decision for him, but I'm glad he relented; I think it gave each runner a deeper sense of sharing the experience, than running along side us could provide.

By mile eighteen, I think it's safe to say we were all hitting the wall. This was close to the course turn around point, and it could not come soon enough, as all of us had reached some level of physical discomfort. This is when, for a brief stretch, we jokingly verbalized our discontent. We hated the sun, we hated the wind charging toward us, we even hated Eric, who pushed us faster, keeping up the pace!

Luckily, this is also nearing the point in the course where we turn toward the ocean on the last leg of the journey. The grandeur and vast majesty of that view, at least for me, seemed to quell the pain to a tolerable level.

The runners say, a marathon is really two races, a twenty miler and a 10k, and I can see why. At mile twenty, the game changes, and it really becomes a mental challenge; the only way through it, is to break it down, into bite size pieces.

The 10k melts into a 5k, and eventually all that stands between you and the finish line, is the final two tenths of a mile. Although I was not running, it seemed that every muscle in my body ached from the inability to move, as badly as it did when I could run, and on some level, I shared the pain of my teammates.

At mile twenty-six, all of them yelled out, "Let's bring this home!", and we lined up across the promenade from side to side, as we crossed the finish line together! This year I intended to earn my medal, and by the end of the race, I felt that I had!

Finish photo from the New Jersey Marathon. Same year as Super Storm Sandy. It was a tough day on all of us. Left to right Meredith, Kyle, Laura, Eric. We always considered these guys family.

I dedicate this blog to my husband Chris, our friends: Meredith, Kyle, Laura and Eric, Nancy, Dani, and Frank, who signed up and smiled through the pain, to help those of us who struggle with ALS every day!

We thank you for your friendship, commitment and generous support; we could not do this without you!

Thank you, my friend Loni, it was an honor to have you and Nathan at the finish line to place my medal around my neck.

Special thanks to Joe Gigas, the Executive Race Director of the New Jersey Marathon, who welcomed us back another year, our friends and family members who's behind the scenes help made this trip possible, and Rob Spahr of the Star-Ledger for picking up our story during ALS awareness month!"

There is such a great parallel between our second NJ Marathon and Denise's condition. Not only was the shore ravaged by Superstorm Sandy, but Denise's body was really wrecked by ALS at this time. That year we raised money not only for the Les Turner Foundation, but also for Restore the Shore, which was near and dear to Denise's heart.

This race had great meaning for Denise. She had such fond memories of the shore and wanted to see all she could. This was also the beginning of incredible discomfort as Denise rode in the race chair, yet in her usual manner she fought through it—as we all did running this marathon.

The shore truly was on the way to recovery by that time, but the remnants of Sandy reared their ugly head as we made our way along the course. During one stretch of the race, around mile 19 or 20, I was pushing the chair through several inches of sand for about an eighth of a mile. Try that during your next leisurely run, let alone twenty miles into one! It may not seem like much, unless you've just run nineteen miles and your entire body is hurting. That was one tough stretch.

Yet, all I could think of as I struggled was, this is nothing compared to what Denise faces each and every minute of every day. So, I just put my head down and got through it.

As we finished, we were all beat up, Denise included. No one was hurting more than Laura; this was her first marathon, and she was, shall we say, "a tad bit undertrained." But we made it, and relished conquering another 26.2. Denise managed to stay awake the whole time, which was one of her goals. Consequently, she felt the pain as much or more than we all did. Her pain lingered beyond ours.

She hurt throughout that night and on the way home too, but she refused to let anything stop her. My hero.

As Denise's condition worsened, her desire to keep doing marathons did not waver. As I've said before, she felt alive when we ran our races. She would grit her teeth through the pain and push on.

Around this time, we were blessed again, as Les Turner purchased us a new race chair from Team Hoyt in Boston to hopefully alleviate the pain Denise was experiencing as I pushed her in both training runs and marathons. It seemed that her back and neck were the source of the majority of the pain.

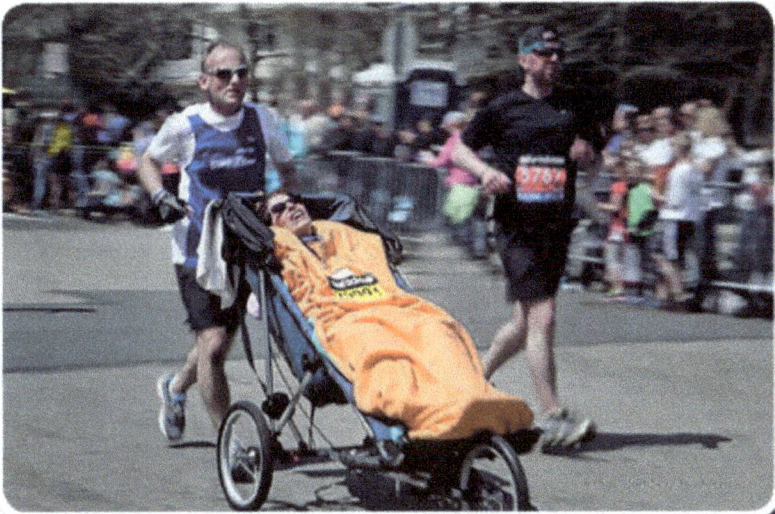

The new chair was phenomenal and so easy to push.
As Denise put it, it was the "Rolls Royce of race chairs,"
not like the "Yugo" we once owned. We had many
great trainings runs and races with the new chair, but
unfortunately it started giving Denise pain and I was on
the phone again to Team Hoyt. They quickly sent us their

"Comfort package," which included pads and devices that could possibly hold Denise's head in a stationary position, support her neck and relieve her back discomfort. Unfortunately, not even this thoughtful array of props seemed to help.

Was this it? Had we finished our last race together?

Let me include a few words about pain. Denise did not have a low threshold for pain. She never let pain stop her and she never complained. So, when we finished one of our races and she said she had been ready to quit early on, I knew I had to do something. Team Hoyt was a godsend.

Team Hoyt had sent the "comfort package" with the understanding that if it didn't wadsttherquicotsthagchschap mehundead dallar dariceuges. Rather,

they woald go with plan B, C, or D, as needed. Obviously, they could have just said,

"Sorry, we've done all we can do," and wash their hands of it. Not Team Hoyt. The people there said, "We're just going to build you a new chair." That was plan B!

Taking into consideration that we drove everywhere we raced, they constructed a chair that came apart and would fit in our van. They promised to have it ready by Boston 2016, just several months after my call for help.

They were true to their word, and on the Saturday before the Boston Marathon (always held on a Monday), we were presented with a new chair. It was ultra-comfortable, and as a result we had a great race, our eighth marathon together. (See Appendix for details on this marvelous piece of workmanship) We were both elated, and it was enjoyable to share a bit of our joy with local media outlets.

As I told Alysha Palumbo of New England Cable News about Denise after the race, "She was amazing. She's, my inspiration. One in

20,000 people survive with ALS and we're in our fifth year. She is my wife, my inspiration. Nothing worth doing should be just a little tough. The marathon was tough on me today, but for me to deal with a rough five hours is nothing compared to what Denise deals with on a daily basis. She is a rock star."

I explained that inspiration to another reporter, WCVB-TV's Juli McDonald:

"It is something I can do to show others living with the disease to not give up your dreams. Just keep setting personal goals."

Denise was thrilled. Her neck and back pain had been alleviated and we looked forward to our next two marathons on the docket: Chicago on October 9th and Naperville on October 23rd.

Denise and I had run to represent the UMass ALS Cellucci Fund, seeking to heighten awareness of ALS and raise funds for breakthrough amyotrophic lateral sclerosis research underway at UMass Medical School. This was actually my fifth Boston marathon, and I have long said that no other race compares to it. It was my second marathon on Beantown with Denise in her chair. We were happy to play our small part in boosting the Cellucci Fund, which was established in 2011 in honor of former Massachusetts Gov. Paul Cellucci, who died from complications of ALS in 2013. In the past several years the fund has generated $3.9 million.

Unfortunately, God had other plans. We would not make it to ten marathons,

Denise's longtime goal. Boston 2016 was our last race together.

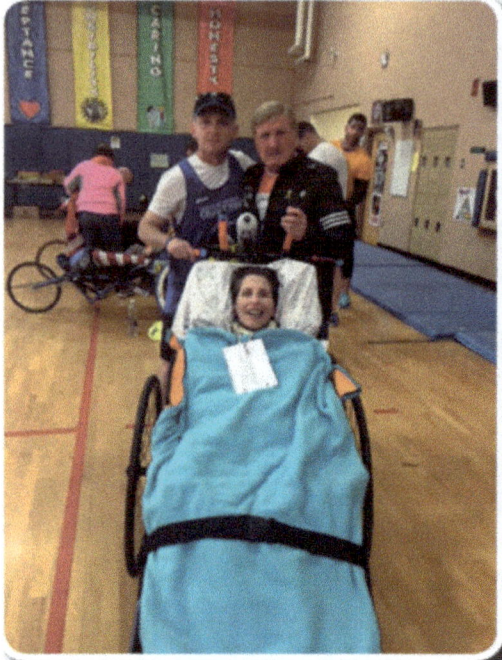

Dick Hoyt had quite a moment with Denise prior to
Boston 2016. What a great man. It's no wonder why
he is such a beloved person in Boston. Amazing.

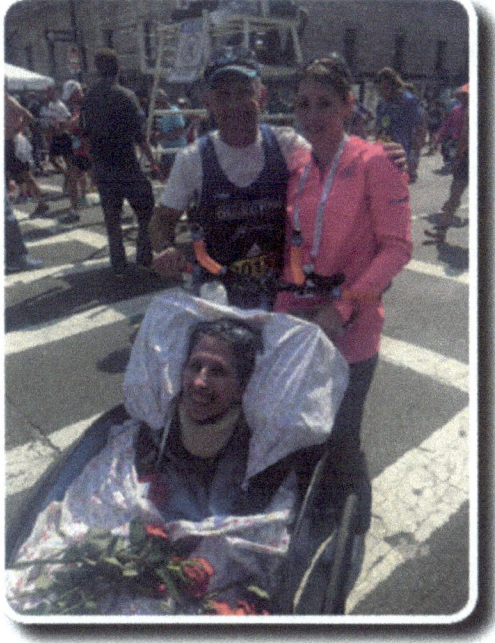

Boston 2016. Our last race together. The girls at Boston College dropped long stem roses in Denise's chair as we went by. So glad Brandi was able to meet us at the finish. I was hurting.

That fact was heartbreaking on many levels. Our prayer for a new, more comfortable chair had been answered, yet it only got to comfort Denise for one race. (See the Appendix for a touching tribute to Denise after her death, written for the UMassMedNow website)

Nonetheless I say, "Thank you, Team Hoyt Racing, and especially Mike DiDonato, for blessing us. You are a credit to all the good you do for all you serve." I did not plan on retiring, however. I will continue to run and raise money to end the nightmare of ALS for others. It's what Denise would want, and I remember her in a special way as I push our "Rolls Royce."

What was it like to push her through eight distance races? Well, "push" is not the right word to use to describe what I did when I ran with Denise in front of me. I never felt burdened. Rather, I felt privileged. I would not have wanted to race alone. I loved Denise's company, I loved making her happy, and I loved raising money for research. That's why "push" is not the right word.

How about "accompanied," or better yet-"propelled." That's it. I propelled Denise, and she propelled me.

"Push" is also not the right word to describe what it was like to race without Denise in her chair. I can't come up with a word to define what I felt running behind an empty chair. I'll let my post for the MDA's "Strongly" site explain:

"One of my most recent marathons was my toughest. Denise and I had planned on running our ninth marathon together on the 9* of October, 2016. But something happened on the way to our golden marathon-Denise passed away, in July 2016. Since that time there hasn't been a lot of happiness in my life; I have just put one foot in front of the other and taken life day by day. Yet, I recalled the promise I had made to Denise to run onward, pushing her chair filled with memories of our life together.

And so I found myself at the starting line of the B of A Chicago Marathon in October 2016, awaiting my 47h race of that length. When Denise passed in the summer, I wasn't sure if I'd ever want to use her race chair again. Then Keri Schindler of Athletes with Disabilities, a subgroup of the Bank of America Chicago Marathon, sent me the nicest e-mail. Keri suggested pushing Denise's empty chair as a tribute to her. I knew if I decided to do it, it would be with MDA Team Momentum •

When I decided I would push Denise's chair, April Tunnicliff and Alison Tibbits of MDA's National Team Momentum group were ecstatic. They could not give me enough support as I planned for the race. They took care of everything to make Chicago 2016 my most memorable run ever. They genuinely cared and were so proud to be part of this new running experience for me, defining grace and beauty as they put my needs (and others') before themselves, just as my Denise did. They blessed me so abundantly on marathon weekend that I will never be able to properly thank them.

I was privileged to have a front row seat to what could only be called a miracle when I took my seat at the Team Momentum Inspiration Dinner on October 8. Talk about a celebration of family! The speakers were phenomenal (I was OK), and April and Alison created a spectacularly beautiful night. I was welcomed with open arms as family, and it was just what I needed then. The way MDA celebrates its own is so uplifting.

On that night I told anyone who would listen, 'MDA is the only charity I will ever run for.' MDA is committed and gets it; it is truly a miracle. The response I received after my speech gave me chills and tears all at once. I felt so part of this family, and it met a huge need in my life.

That night after the dinner, I didn't sleep much before race day. I was still a bundle of nerves as I hopped into the cab and headed for the gym where all Team Momentum runners would meet. I was early because I was with the Athletes with Disabilities group and needed to be staged and checked in by 6:15 a.m. I was not sure who was going to be there to meet me.

Of course, April and Alison were there to greet me with big hugs.

My nerves subsided after getting to the gym. Alison even escorted me to the start because I had no clue where I was going. As I waited with the other participants, I started feeling strange. I'm not disabled, and everyone around me was. I felt guilty, like I shouldn't have been there. This trepidation stopped when a veteran who lost his legs in battle came up to me and said he had seen a

TV segment about my decision to push Denise's chair. He put his fist to his heart a couple times and said 'much respect.' That did wonders for me.

I stood there with Denise's chair holding only her photo and a couple of medals from marathons that we had done. I realized again that I would need to draw freely on Denise's spirit and positivity to reach the finish line, given my imminent exhaustion and emotional state. I remembered what I had told the WLS affiliate in Chicago about Denise: 'If I could be half the person she was, it would be a success, it would be a successful life. But I miss her. I miss her terribly. I know she'll be with us on marathon day and she'll see to it that I get through safely.'

The actual race was a roller coaster of emotions for me. After all, Denise was supposed to have raced with me. The tears came on multiple occasions when I thought of that. I laughed at some signs people held. I smiled as random strangers yelled my name and called me a hero and an inspiration. What blew my mind was that my name was nowhere on my bib or shirt. How did they know who I was? The WLS TV segment had aired at 5:30 a.m. the day before. Miracle!

My body held up fairly well until mile 18, when calf cramps started. I was still a long way out. As I stopped to stretch before mile 19, I was preparing for a long 7.2 miles in. I'm not sure what happened, but I think Denise had something to do with it as those last 7.2 flew by with nary a twinge of a cramp.

I also ran into a bunch of Team Momentum teammates and we chatted a bit.

And then something happened, and it was beautiful. Early in the race, I thought about doing something special at the end for Denise. I wanted it to be clear that the Chicago Marathon was not about me, it was about keeping Denise's spirit alive as we did something she loved. So, I decided when I hit mile 26 that I would get Denise's picture out of her chair and hold it in my left hand as I crossed the finish line, the love of my life truly with me.

This gesture awakened the finish line crowd-it exploded as we finished. I think the people realized there was something bigger transpiring than a 26.2-mile jaunt through the city. When I was in the finish chute, volunteers stopped what they were doing and clapped for me. I, of course was in tears, and when Keri approached me with tears in her eyes and hugged me, I absolutely lost it. She thanked me for doing the marathon. I thought: I should be thanking her.

I met up with my buddies in the marathon's VIP tent and had a great moment with them (yes, it did include a few cold ones). They will be joining me in New Jersey one last time next April to run with Denise. They told me they had been deeply moved when they saw me finish. They were proud, as so many people have been around the country when Denise and I raced together. As one person summarized his feelings: 'Watching the two of you set such an amazing example to the rest of us on unwavering faith, strength, courage, determination and most of all love, has been so inspiring.' We repeatedly heard sentiments like this one, and it inspired to continue our trek for as long as Denise was alive-and beyond, now.

On that morning in Chicago, I finally I headed back to the Team Momentum meeting area in the gym. So many people greeted me and shared stories of the day.

I love the closeness of this Team Momentum group and I feel so fortunate to be part of the MDA family. I hope to be an active member for many years to come.

God blessed me when I was introduced to Team Momentum.

Miracle!"

CHAPTER 6

The Last Post

I'll close this book with Denise's last blog and a few reflections of my own. Before you get a final look at her beautiful soul, I wanted to share a quote from her that rings in my ears and reminds me of what kind of person she was. Just before we did the 2016 Boston Marathon, the Granddaddy of all marathons, Denise remarked on her good fortune of living beyond the five-year mark after being diagnosed with ALS. Get this: only one in 20,000 ALS patients lives that long. I told you she was extraordinary!

Denise, despite knowing that her end was drawing nearer, blurted out,

"Finally, I'm above average at something!" Anyone who knew her knew that she was way above average in all things. Way above average.

And, her posts were far above the norm as well. As our racing career had heated up, Denise's writing career had wound down. It was simply too difficult for her to keep up even a two-post-per-month pace. That's why her last posts are so precious. They were some of the last words that Denise ever penned.

The fact that Denise was able to write at all, given the destructive nature of ALS, was remarkable to me. At this point in time, she had absolutely no use of her hands. Her neck muscles were weakened, and even keeping her head up enough to use her Dynavox was acutely painful. Many times, I'd leave her alone to write, and fifteen minutes later I'd find her crying at the screen because she couldn't do it.

This was so frustrating for someone as strong-willed as Denise, and it was heartbreaking for the rest of us too. She loved blogging, and she felt she was making a difference in the lives of others as she faced down this disease. She fought through her posts just as she fought ALS for five plus years. Nothing was going to stop her from posting on events that impacted her both positively and negatively.

Often, Denise would start writing, then fall asleep as the effort drained her completely. Yet, she refused to let ALS rob her of another passion until she was completely unable to power through even a short blog. Denise had more perseverance than anyone I know. She was a gift. I will never be able to put in in words or do justice to what it took for Denise to blog three to four years into this disease. It was, in a word, mind-boggling.

She wrapped up her writing career with this beauty as she looked forward to her inevitable destiny.

"Thing I Miss," penned June 23, 2013:

"Disclaimer: the following litany of activities is in no order of priority, they are, as they fall haphazardly into my mind and onto the screen before me. It is, in fact, incomplete, as I'm certain that once posted, I'm apt to recall something I have neglected to include. It also excludes those things that are private, and should remain so...

I would also like to point out that I do not intend to present this as a list of complaints, it is simply one individual's perspective of living with restrictions, in the spirit of Julie Andrews, let's try to think of it as a list of some of My Favorite Things.

Hugging, don't underestimate the power of human touch.

I come from an Italian family, and we're huggers; we hug our friends, their friends, relatives, co-workers, acquaintances, and pretty much anyone who evokes the natural urge in us.

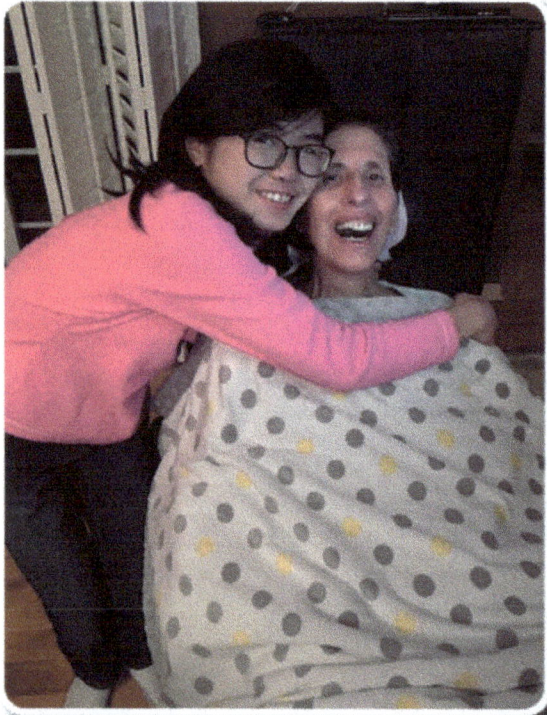

Maddie giving her mom one of her patented
awesome hugs. No one hugs like Maddie.

While I still receive hugs, my arms are not strong enough to wrap around anyone and hug back, so while I still enjoy them, I feel like something is missing. I've also noticed, the hugs I receive are much gentler. I know I'm not looking very strong, but I assure you, I won't break from a more robust hug if you are so inclined. My daughter is proof of that as she often embraces me with the approach of a wrestler attacking his opponent, and I have managed to survive.

Driving, after more than a decade of commuting in bumper-to-bumper traffic to get to work, I can hardly believe I'm saying this but I miss driving. There is just something about the freedom that I felt when I was driving alone on a sunny day, with the sunroof open blasting my favorite music. Yes, of course I was singing along, and there were times, my hands may have left the steering wheel as I made a joyful noise...

Shopping, I know what you're thinking, what woman doesn't like to shop and well... I can still shop online or go to the store in my power wheelchair. It's just not the same. Shopping was therapeutic, relaxing, and though I avoided malls, I enjoyed taking a leisurely stroll through Target on Sunday with my husband, Chris.

Although, he insisted on having a list, and imposed a maximum number of impulse purchases, sometimes putting a damper on the excursion. It was all in good fun, as I rarely got reigned in for exceeding the limit.

Movies, yes, I can still go to the movies, but the experience is not quite the same...

Handicapped seating is safely located at floor level, you know this area as the place you have to sit if you arrive late to a popular movie on Saturday night. It can be hard on the neck, unless of course you have a Permobile C-300 with tilt controls!

While I can see the logic, I really miss the view I might otherwise enjoy in the upper rows of stadium seating! Refreshment options are also limited, as I want to be considerate of my fellow patrons, and spare them the delight of spontaneous aspiration on a rogue kernel of popcorn. Luckily, the popcorn at our local theater smells better than it actually tastes.

Rollerblading, one of my greatest passions! There were times when I thought my feet could literally leave the pavement as I experienced the joy of skating! I could circle the neighborhood repeatedly in the early hours of a summer day listening to Casting Crowns, Chris Tomlin, Third Day and a variety of other Christian rock groups. I can clearly remember raising my arms in sheer joy and gratitude for the pleasure it gave me, acknowledging it as a gift. Who knows what the neighbors thought, as the crazy middle-aged woman raced by, while they sipped their morning coffee from their decks overlooking the lake...? I am still grateful that I have those memories to meditate on as I sit here.

Singing, I enjoyed singing from an early age and later with my daughter, Maddie.

We would have shown tunes pouring from the iPod dock most mornings, and sing and dance as we got moving, a trick I learned that often helped get a sleepy toddler up and ready to embrace the day! We still enjoy music together but I'm leaving the singing to Maddie, and it still brings me joy knowing it's a passion we share.

Cycling, I logged many miles along the Prairie Path and the Great Western Trail over the past decade and a half, and I really miss that too. The smell of the woods always reminded me of camping with my dad and siblings, I could hardly get enough of it as I breathed in deeply, filling my lungs to push my legs as fast as they could go. Racing past the trees, ducking from the lower branches, and drinking in the colors of the prairie grass and goldenrod against the deep blue sky. I was experiencing heaven on earth.

Cross country skiing with my husband Chris, a sport we took up together the winter after we met. Chris had been teaching it for years at school with the kids, but really wasn't doing it for fun outside of school. First, we started out in the open spaces behind our home with the girls; it was a fun family activity, and then we branched out to actually buying gear, and finding trails to explore.

It was peaceful in the woods, gliding along together, enjoying the wildlife as we spotted deer, bunnies, and field mice... Actually, I recall several dead field mice along the prairie path, still scratching my head over that...?

My favorite memory of this was our trip to Hickory Hideaway for Valentine's Day weekend! Chris rented a log cabin and we ski'd at Lake Carol Country Club! It was pretty hilly out that way, and we had a few scary moments as it challenged us a bit beyond our skill level, but I enjoyed every bit of it!

Physical activities with my husband and our girls, I miss skating and cross-country skiing with them, riding the waves in the ocean, playing in the pool and snow tubing, the list goes on... While I have never been much of a spectator, I can still enjoy watching them! My favorite is watching all three of them compete in Dance Party on the Wii. I'm certain Chris will deny it, but I have video proof!

Work, I loved my job, and the people I had the pleasure of working with! I had the opportunity to challenge myself, and my team to continually look for ways to improve the process. I had the best team of people; they often taught me more than I taught them. I'm grateful that I had the kind of job that I was excited to be at every day!

Dressing up, at the risk of sounding vain, I must admit I miss the dresses, the heels, the feeling of being comfortable in my own skin! We attended a very special wedding this weekend, and while I got to wear a dress, pretty patent leather flats, and some jewelry, my body just barely held the dress up. I just don't look like myself anymore... Yes, it's vanity, but its also a feeling of confidence. I was completely stressed, out worrying about how I looked, whether I could keep it together through the ceremony, and not become a spectacle as I often cry at weddings. I didn't want to be the woman sobbing in her wheelchair disrupting the ceremony.

It was also awkward to have my speech device attached to my chair outside of my home to attend this kind of event, but I needed it to communicate. Turns out everything went smoothly, Chris took super good care of me, everyone made me feel comfortable; I even enjoyed a few sips of wine, totally relaxing me, and had a wonderful time!

So, to sum it up, life is different but it's still good, and I'm thankful for the memories, they are vivid in my mind and this disease cannot take them from me..."

A glamour shot on our Honeymoon Cruise to Jamaica.
She is so beautiful.
This is how we should remember Denise.

As you can tell from this book, this confrontation with ALS was one long walk of faith. Denise and I were put in a situation we wouldn't wish on anyone. It is a testament to our faith and Denise's legacy that we were able to make the best of it.

It was proof positive that faith can move mountains.

We were fortunate to have a great support network of family and friends.

Although at times it seemed we were in this alone, we never walked even a step alone. We have only God to thank for that. He put people in our life at certain times to help us to navigate the often-bumpy road. In the words of one of my favorite Chris Tomlin songs, "Our God is a good, good God."

If you find yourself in a situation like ours, try and remember you are not alone-ever. God doesn't give us what we can handle; he helps us handle what we are given. People are good and they want to help. Our world is good, even though the bad is what is mostly covered in the news. Be brave as you stare down your particular situation. You are not alone. Our God is there and will see to it that you get through.

In the past eighteen months I have delivered a eulogy for my wife and two older brothers. God got me through that. He will get you through your situation.

Try to do some good even when the situation seems hopeless, but most of all remember that the road you travel can and will impact others. Will it be in a good or bad way? You decide.

My hope is that this book impacts you in a way that makes a difference in your life. Just as Denise impacted my life in such a phenomenal way.

Thank you.

Perhaps a few words I shared in a blog post for MDA's "Strongly" site best summarizes my journey with Denise during our brief marriage and our memorable runs together: "I was so blessed to find Denise and make her my wife. If I could marry Denise tomorrow, knowing full well that ALS would rear its ugly head, without hesitation I would marry her again. That's how I roll."

Her chair may be empty, but my heart is not.

In fact, Denise DiMarzo will remain forever in the hearts of hundreds of people who knew and loved her.

I hope and pray she will remain in yours as well.

Appendix

(I think a reprint of this entire article here would be great)

http://www.dailyherald.com/article/20120516/news/705169943/

Reprint of this article as well:

http://www.umassmed.edu/news/news-archives/2014/04/boston-marathoners-run-for-the-cellucci-fund/

Reprint of this article:

http://www.umassmed.edu/news/news-archives/2016/04/custom-wheelchair-to-aid-umass-als-cellucci-fund-duo-at-boston-marathon/

Reprint of this:

http://www.umassmed.edu/news/news-archives/2016/04/newsmakers-umass-als-cellucci-fund-duo-complete-2016-boston-marathon/

Reprint:

http://www.umassmed.edu/news/news-archives/2016/08/umass-als-cellucci-fund-marathoner-denise-dimarzo-succumbs-to-als/_

http://www.dodgin4lougehrigs.com/

About The Author

Denise DiMarzo is the inspiration for this book. Her blogs are riveting and we see her strength throughout this work. She put Jesus first and everything after that a distant second even as ALS ravaged her body. The first to help someone in need and raised infinite awareness for ALS patients. She was and is my wife, my hero, my inspiration.

Chris Benyo is an elementary PE teacher and has been teaching for twenty-eight years. He is not a writer. He is an avid runner and has completed forty-seven marathons to date, eight of which he completed while pushing the love of his life Denise. Together Chris and Denise raised over 150K for ALS awareness and patient care with the help of so many friends and family members.

www.ingramcontent.com/pod-product-compliance
Lightning Source LLC
Chambersburg PA
CBHW052115030426
42335CB00025B/2999